CORE ENGLISH

Feeling Different

CORE ENGLISH

Feeling Different

Anne Mitchell, Anne Rigg,
Ronald Caie and Hellen Matthews

SERIES EDITOR:
Colin Lamont

HEINEMANN EDUCATIONAL BOOKS

Heinemann Educational Books Ltd
22 Bedford Square, London WC1B 3HH

LONDON EDINBURGH MELBOURNE AUCKLAND
HONG KONG SINGAPORE KUALA LUMPUR NEW DELHI
IBADAN NAIROBI JOHANNESBURG PORTSMOUTH (NH)
KINGSTON

First published 1985
Reprinted 1985

British Library Cataloguing in Publication Data

Core English
  Feeling different.
  1. English literature—20th century
  I. Lamont, Colin   II. Mitchell, Ann
  820.8′00912   PR1148

  ISBN 0-435-10580-9

Designed and typeset by Leaper and Gard Ltd, Bristol
Printed and bound in Great Britain

CONTENTS

Dead Smart
One of the Boys

My name . . . Well that don't matter
But I goes to this 'ere school,
And I've got a reputation
For breaking every rule.
The teachers they all hate me,
Every master I annoys,
'Cos I'm a right old criminal –
Dead smart, one of the boys.

The first day at me new school
Me teacher got right shocked,
'Cos straight away I lost me cap –
That's how the lav. got blocked!
And I burns me new school blazer
Hiding gaspers[1] in me pocket,
And I decides, in this 'ere boat,
It's me is gonna rock it.

Next day the form's dead eager
As through the gates they swarm,
And they elects some swotty clot
As captain of the form.
Now so far I've gone easy,
Just sizing up the dump,
But when I sees what that job's worth,
I gives that clot a clump.

So he resigns, and after
I've persuaded all the rest,
I gets elected. Then I starts
To feather my own nest.
I helps with dinner money –
Of course I takes my cut –
The teacher couldn't work it out,

[1] gaspers: cigarettes.

And he promptly done his nut,
So the teachers they all hate me,
Every master I annoys,
'Cos I'm a right old criminal –
Dead smart, one of the boys.

You lot goes to Assembly,
But me, I'm never there.
I sits and has a crafty smoke
Down the – well, you know where.
Then I copies some kid's homework,
And if I gets found out,
I makes him say he copied mine,
Or I punch him on the snout.

So as my innocent years roll by
I'm in on every racket,
And anyone who tries it on,
He quickly cops a packet!

Till in the fourth year I can claim
To be the school's real boss.
And I spends me time in dodging work,
'Cos work, that's a dead loss.
So the teachers, they all hate me,
Every master I annoys,
'Cos I'm a right old criminal –
Dead smart, one of the boys.

Our form gets up a football team,
Of course I wasn't picked.
So when they left the field they found
Their money had been nicked.
But though they're all dead stupid,
They guessed I'd had a go,
So when I tries to talk to them,
They just don't want to know.

Then last week, down the billiard hall,
I joins up with a mob,
And we breaks into some radio shop –
A very crafty job,
Till some dirty copper spots us,
And I'm the one gets caught,
And there's no-one who'll stand by me
Next week when I'm in court.

And you can't help feeling rotten,
When you stand about and wait
For some bloke who'll say 'Hello' to you
But there's no-one who's your mate.
And when the rest all live it up,
There's no-one thinks of me.
But I don't care. When I'm big time
I'll show you – wait and see.

All you teachers, you what hates me,
Every master I annoys,
'Cos I'm a right old criminal . . .
Dead smart . . . One of the boys . . .

William Samson

3

Nooligan

I'm a nooligan
dont give a toss
in our class
I'm the boss
(well, one of them)

I'm a nooligan
got a nard 'ead
step out of line
and youre dead
(well, bleedin)

I'm a nooligan
I spray me name
all over town
footballs me game
(well, watchin)

I'm a nooligan
violence is fun
gonna be a nassassin
or a nired gun
(well, a soldier)

Roger McGough

3

Three Fingers are Plenty

When I was a child I was dominated by a boy I shall call Kirk. I was brought up in a proud old town on the Moray Firth coast of Scotland, and I was brought up in the North Scottish Presbyterian way, that is, Very Properly Indeed. I have never really understood, therefore, why I was allowed to make a friend of Kirk, for Kirk was far from proper. He was a kind of Scotch Huckleberry Finn – a boy who went barefoot, wore orra patched breeks[1], smoked a clay cutty[2], chewed plug tobacco, jeuked[3] the school. By all the standards of our time and place, Kirk was beyond the pale. He even worked on Sundays.

Kirk lived with Baggie McLaughlin and his hairy old wife in the cottage at the foot of our hill. Baggie was a small wizened man who touched his forelock to everyone, even me aged eight, and always walked on the grass verge of the road. He called himself a pig-sticker. He went round the out-lying crofts at Martinmas, killing off the pigs at a shilling a time, and this was the only work he ever admitted to. In fact, he was a beachcomber. Kirk used sometimes to say that he was a retired pirate, but I knew quite well that this was an exaggeration. Baggie would not have said boo to a gosling.

His wife was very old. I suppose she must have been about the same age as Baggie, but she looked much older. She was crippled with arthritis, bent like a right angle, and heavily bearded. She rose late and retired early, and when she wanted to go to bed she would hobble to the cottage door and ring a big ship's bell that Baggie had picked off the shore, and then Kirk had to run home and help get her into bed. He said it was a hell of a job getting her into bed, and I bet it was, for she was solid as teak and must have weighed close on sixteen stone.

As far as anybody knew, Kirk had lived all his life with this old couple, but even I, who had no biological knowledge, knew that he did not belong to them. He was of different

---

[1]orra patched breeks: odd patched trousers.
[2]cutty: short pipe.
[3]jeuked: dodged.

stock. He looked every man in the eye and touched his forelock to none. As I remember him he was tall for his age,
straight as a mast, flat-backed, and uncommonly broad
across the shoulders. His hair was red, and he wore it very
long, except when Baggie put a bowl on top of it and cut
round the rim, and then he was a sorry sight – but nobody
ever laughed at him. At least, no boy did.

The most remarkable thing about him was his eyes. I
never noticed the colour of anyone else's eyes until I grew up
and started looking at girls, but I could not help noticing
Kirk's. They were greenish-blue, the colour of blue-bottle
flies in the sun, and they were full of devil. When Kirk flicked
me with those blue-bottle eyes of his and said, 'What are we
waiting for?' I just automatically said, 'Let's go.' I always
said it, and I always went. I guess I'd have gone anywhere at
all with Kirk.

Kirk was a year and nine months older than me. When he
was ten he built a boat out of three-ply wood and petrol-
cans, and we sailed this boat on the open sea. We were often
afloat for the whole day, and sometimes we went so far out
to sea that we lost sight of land. When it blew up we shipped
a lot of water, and then I baled like fury with two Rowntree
cocoa tins while Kirk sat cross-legged in the stern, keeping
her bows up to the seas by judicious management of his oar
(my sister's tennis racket with the gut out and a sheet of tin
nailed in its place). He was never at a loss, never rattled –
never afraid – and twenty years ago I had much the same
degree of confidence in Kirk and his three-ply *Ruler of the
Waves* as I now have in Captain Illingworth and the *Queen
Mary.*

One day during an aquatic gala in the harbour of a small
town nine or ten miles up the coast, Kirk paddled through
the bottle-neck into the basin, and allowed himself to be
captured by the judges' launch. When they asked where he
had come from, he pointed out to sea and said, 'Norge.' The
local folks made a great fuss of him, presented him to Lady
somebody or other who was there for the prize-giving, fed
him on chocolate and ice-cream, and billeted him with the
Minister. The Minister had then three young daughters – one
of whom is now my wife – and she has told me that Kirk
made such a powerful impression, what with slapping his
chest, emitting guttural growls, and declaiming, 'Ach so?'
that she and her sisters were all slightly in love with him for
weeks.

The imposture lasted less than a day, but it happened to be the day the weekly county paper went to press, and our normally reliable journal came out with a sober account of Kirk's adventure under the heading, 'Young Viking's Exploit'.

In due course Kirk and his boat were sent home in one of Alexander's big blue buses, the story was the talk of the town, and my father, discovering that I had sometimes gone to sea with Kirk, thrashed me judicially and, with an axe over his shoulder, marched me down to Baggie's cottage, where he fulminated against Kirk and duly despatched the boat. It is characteristic of Kirk that while my father was telling Baggie exactly what he meant to do to *that boy* if ever he laid hands on him, that boy was grinning smugly down at us from a branch not six feet above my father's head.

Kirk was always one jump ahead of the other fellow. I am sure that was the secret of his leadership. When a gang of us went guddling[4], Kirk would coax a whole frying of sizeable trout into his thick fingers while the rest of us puddled with a few miserable sticklebacks. If we went along the cliffs to rob gulls' nests, it was Kirk who spotted the best colonies and only Kirk who would dare climb to them. It was Kirk who first showed us a bowline on the bight and a Turk's head, who made fish-hooks for us out of horse-shoe nails, who taught us to lift and *cope* a ferret, who assembled the radio for our Ku-Klux clubroom. He was a born leader. He was always out

[4]guddling: catching fish with one's hands, without a rod or net.

in front, and whenever there was anything important to be done it was always Kirk who did it best.

The people of my home town still talk about Kirk's jumping.

The first time he jumped from the Brig o'Doom was one Sunday afternoon when he would have been about twelve. We had gone for a walk, the pair of us, and we were leaning over the parapet of the Brig looking for salmon swirls in the pool some sixty feet below when Kirk said, 'Bet you couldn't jump it.' I said, 'Bet you couldn't either,' and Kirk jumped it.

When I told them at school they wouldn't believe me, and I laid bets wholesale, and the following Saturday the whole school turned up to see Kirk jump from the Brig again. Everybody was scared stiff when he climbed up on the parapet, but after it was all over some of the older boys said it was easy enough that side, they'd like to see him do it on the other side, between the rocks, *that's* where they had bet he wouldn't jump. So Kirk jumped on the other side, between the rocks, and while he was jumping Alan Maxwell fainted, and at least half of us didn't dare look. Kirk said it was easy, he would jump it any time we wanted, but none of us who had seen him do it wanted to see him do it again. Of course there were some who had missed the fun, and so for several Saturdays Kirk, accompanied by bands of boys, went out to Doom, and for a collection of pennies, marbles, chewing-gum, etc., jumped from the Brig.

Next it was the Town Bridge. I don't know who first threw out the challenge by saying it was impossible to jump from the Town Bridge, it might have been any of us, for – goodness knows – we all knew very well how impossible it was. The Town Bridge is even higher than Doom, and there isn't more than five or six feet of water at the deepest point.

Kirk was to jump at ten o'clock on a Saturday morning, and by nine o'clock there was such a press of boys on the bridge that traffic was at a standstill, there were hooting lines of cars at both ends, and the police were out in force trying to move us on. When Kirk appeared, Sergeant Munro, I think it was, collared him and led him by the scruff of the neck to the police station. Kirk said he had a bad time in the police station, he didn't exactly get the third degree, but he had a thoroughly bad time; he was told all about Borstal, and he was told that he would be sent there, broken neck and all, if he ever dared jump from the Town Bridge. They kept him in the police station for over an hour, and when Kirk came

out he said he would be there still if he hadn't finally promised, Scout's honour, that he wouldn't jump from the bridge.

Well, Kirk didn't jump.

He dived, and he got off lightly, breaking only his left arm and collar-bone and cracking open his skull across his two crowns.

He wasn't sent to Borstal, but he spent five weeks on his back in Palmer's Hospital.

When Kirk was thirteen Baggie said it was time he stopped scrimshanking[5] and learned a trade. Actually Kirk had worked at odd jobs from the time he was able to walk – lifting potatoes[6], picking rasps, delivering papers and groceries, shovelling coke in the gasworks, helping mysteriously in the blacksmith's shop, and so on – but of course there wasn't any future in these jobs, and I suppose that Baggie was thinking only of what was best for Kirk when he decided to apprentice him to Old John Low, the tailor.

Kirk felt terrible about it. He said flatly that he wasn't going to be a tailor. He wasn't going to do woman's work in a stuffy shop, not him; he had set his heart on the sea, and he was going to sea and be damned to them all. There were some desperate scenes in the cottage at the foot of the hill,

[5]scrimshanking: shirking his duty.
[6]lifting potatoes: picking potatoes.

and after one of them, when Baggie had thrashed him with a strap, Kirk ran away. He was caught in Aberdeen on board an Icelandic trawler and sent home, and he spent exactly one day at work in the tailor's shop. On the evening of that day Baggie came up to our house and, with a great flurry of lock-touching, asked to see my father.

'It's about ma loon[7], Kirk,' he said, panting.

'Fit's wrang wi' your loon?[8]' our maid asked.

'Ma loon's took the chopper and chopped off his thimble finger,' Baggie said.

My father listened in amazement to the story and gave his advice. His advice was to send the boy to sea, and the sooner the better.

Kirk was duly sent to sea and disappeared from my life. I wrote him twice, addressing my letters to the Assistant Cook aboard the trawler *Esmeralda*, c/o the Aberdeen Trawling Company, but I did not get any reply. I have not seen Kirk since that day nearly twenty years ago when he came to say good-bye with all his worldly possessions in a small sack on his back and his right hand still in bandages.

But although I have not seen him I have thought of him often. At moments of crisis my mind seems always to have returned to Kirk, and I am deeply conscious of having hitched my wagon to the stars which he, in childhood, showed me. It was Kirk who taught me by his example that a man must be true to himself, no matter what the cost, and that lesson has stood me in good stead at all the cross-roads in my life. It was because of Kirk's example that I dug my heels in and insisted that I was going to be a writer, not a doctor. It was because of Kirk that, when war broke out, I chose to go to sea rather than join Naval Intelligence and sit in an office job ashore. And then, during the war, when things happened to me – when my ship was blown up under me in the North Sea, when I was attacked by a pack of U-boats on Atlantic convoy, and when I swept five mines in twenty minutes off Normandy on D-day minus one – it was mainly because I had moulded my life on Kirk that I was able to behave, in these testing moments, in a way that I like to think was adequate. Again and again I have found myself thinking of that red-headed boy, imagining him as a much-decorated fighter pilot, as a parachutist on a hopeless mission, as the

[7]ma loon: my boy.
[8]Fit's wrang wi' your loon?: What's wrong with your boy?

leader of a suicidal guerrilla band, and whenever I have felt my spirits flag, when I have been faced with a problem that has seemed too big for me, I have summoned up a picture of Kirk and I have asked myself, 'What would *he* do?' And of course the thing that Kirk would do has always been the thing which has been most difficult for me to do, but it has also been the right thing – and once in a while I've done it.

I owe Kirk a debt that I can never repay.

Although I have not seen him since we were boys together, I *have* heard of him. On Christmas Eve, 1945, when we were clearing the last of the Mediterranean minefields, a Sammy mine popped up underneath my ship and blew her stern off. We were towed into Algiers, and those officers who had lost their gear went ashore to find a tailor.

They found a very good one in a little shop off the *place du Gouvernement*, a genial and characterful Scotsman who had lost a finger fighting pirates in the China Seas. They were pleased with the gear he sold them, and they brought back his card and stuck it on the wardroom notice-board. It read:

> KIRK McLAUGHLIN
> European Tailor
>
> 75 rue Bab Azoun
> Algiers
>
> CLASSY CLOTHES FOR CLASSY
> GENTS

It was unmistakably Kirk.

Neil Paterson

4

Out of Place

So alone
In a place
So crowded
So lost
In a place
Well known.
So young
In a generation
Not mine.
So blue
When all colours
Are red.
So tired
When the sun
Dissolves the sky.
So dead
In the land
Of the living.

Colin Smith

It may be found necessary to apply a second coat

He was
A wild young man
He couldn't care
For what they thought, or said –
He had his own ideas.
His looks provoked his father to protest:
'In my young days
A man who dressed like *that*
Was not a man.'
His mother grew afraid
Of this fierce strange young man
– Her son.

He's all right now
He has 'improved' with age
'I knew it – just a passing phase
They all go through,'
His mother smiles.
He's got a good, safe job,
A wife, a lawn-mower . . .
He's alright now.

Lesley Rigg

Maladjusted Boys

I have made ten minutes of silence.
I know they are afraid of silence
And the mind's pattern of order.
They gaze at me out of oblique faces
And try to fidget away the bleak thoughts
Simmering in the dark tangle of their minds.
I read their unfriendly eyes, cushion
The confused hatred, stand presumptuously
And pretend not to be afraid.
I keep at them with my eyes,
Will them to work and ride
The storm in a roomful of cold attention.
Here and there faces cringe
And I read a future . . . the dark corner
Of a street hiding the cruel
Thud of a chain or boot.
I see a hunter mask glow on a face
And grimy nailbitten hands bend a ruler
To its limit . . . all this in a room
Yellow with June sun and music
Of birds from a private wood.

Robert Morgan

Dragon in the Garden

EXTRACT 1

I'd never seen Cronton School until the morning I started there. My mother took me in the car, dropping me at the gate.

She grinned at me and said, 'Now it's up to you.'

I walked straight in, looking forward in an odd, excited way to being the same as other kids. The school was just as my mother had described it, a grouping of shoe-box shapes made of concrete and glass, with the brilliant green of an overgrown playing-field stretching away behind it towards the distance where the hills were.

I walked along the front of the school and round a corner and I was in the playground. In front of me were hundreds of boys doing the things I had never done. They were wrestling and rolling and screaming and shouting. They were darting and dashing so swiftly that the patterns of their movements made me dizzy, while their noise deafened me.

In a corner of the playground I met loneliness for the first time in my life. Loneliness isn't being alone but wondering why you have to be alone. I had rarely known other kids, I had always been alone, yet in those first moments at school I felt loneliness flood through me as I watched the hundreds of boys. My brain ached as their uproar beat against it. They and I were all wearing the same uniform, but they were different from me. They were rough savages, screaming their war-cries and rushing into brutal battle, and they were happy in a way I had never known. They were happy shouting at each other, wrestling each other, hating each other.

Then one of them spotted me and, like a dog catching a strange scent, he swerved and stopped in front of me. He was smaller than I was and younger and his thick glasses gave him the look of an owl.

'You a new kid?' he asked.

I nodded.

'What's your name?'

'Stewart,' I said. He was shooting his questions at me like

bullets and I didn't like them.

'Stewart what?' he asked.

'Jimmy Stewart.'

'Jimmy Stewart,' he said as if tasting the name. Then he went into a convulsive dance and started screaming, *'Jimmy Stewpot! Jimmy Stewpot!'*

I was so astonished that I just stared at him and didn't at first see the other boys his voice had attracted. They came gathering round and while he went on jerking like a Dervish[1] they studied me. He was red-faced and hoarse, his spectacles were on the end of his nose, he was a nightmare of a boy yet they watched me.

'He's a new kid!' he yelled. 'His name's Jimmy Stewpot!'

I could see dozens of pairs of eyes and I knew how zoo animals must feel on Sunday afternoons when people press close to the cages. There was a dull kind of interest in all the eyes; interest and animosity, but no friendliness. I felt lonelier than ever.

Reginald Maddock

[1]Dervish: an order of Mohammedan friars, famed for their dancing and howling.

Dragon in the Garden

EXTRACT 2

I was in a new world. I went through strange alien rites. I
met the Headmaster and an oldish woman who lived in the
lavender-scented atmosphere of an office next to the Head's.
They asked me questions and wrote in books and, when it
was over, the lavender secretary took me through the school,
chattering to me endlessly and only stopping when we met a
master, a small bustling man with a black gown and a bristly
moustache.

'Mr Harris!' she sang.

He scowled and said nothing.

'A new boy for you, Mr Harris,' she said. 'James Stewart.
Mr Mason says he'll have a word with you later.'

Mr Harris didn't even look at me. He said, 'Wait in my
room, boy,' and walked away.

The lavender secretary whispered, 'It's the room at the
end,' and went clicking along the corridor in pursuit of him.

I found the room at the end of the corridor. Its door was
open and there was an excited noise inside it. As soon as I
went in the noise stopped, switched off. The boys stared at
me, and a paper aeroplane, floating in the air, slid unheeded
to the floor.

'It's that new kid,' somebody said. 'Old Mason's put him
in 2E.'

'Charlie isn't going to like that,' somebody else said. 'It'll
give him more marking than ever.'

There must have been thirty boys sitting mostly in pairs at
desks. I'd never seen so many boys in one tight group. I
stood out there at the front, exposed and solitary, and I saw
them as thirty segments of one body.

'They call him "Stewpot",' one of them said. 'Specky Miller
out of 1R christened him.'

There was a titter.

'Fagso Brown's going to have him seen to,' another of
them said, and there was a groan.

Near to me, at the front of the class, was a red-haired boy
with eyes as blue as innocence.

'You better watch out for Fagso, kid,' he said. 'Fagso's tough. He's tougher than any kid in school. You're O.K. if you're one of his boys, but you watch out if you aren't.'

The boy next to him slowly poked his inkwell with a pencil. He nodded. He was bigger than the other boys in the room and his hair was so close-cropped that his scalp shone through it.

'There's three you've got to watch out for,' he said. 'Fagso, old Mason and Charlie Harris.'

'Charlie's the worst of the teachers!' somebody called from the back of the room and there was an instant's uneasy silence while they all listened for footsteps in the corridor.

'Charlie's dead easy if you know how,' the red-haired boy said. 'How about if we tell the new kid? How about if we help him a bit? Then he won't have to suffer like we did.'

One or two of the boys wriggled and grinned and somebody said, 'You tell him, Ginger! Go on!'

The big boy said, 'You'll be O.K., Evans. Fagso'll look after you.'

Ginger's smile and voice were smooth. 'It's like this, kid. Charlie Harris is our Form Master. You seen him yet? A little chap with a 'tache and a face like sudden death?'

I nodded. 'I saw him in the corridor.'

'Posh!' Ginger said. 'Talks like that chap on the telly, this kid!'

'Get on with it!' the big boy growled at him. 'You were on about Charlie Harris. It was your idea.'

'You saw Charlie, kid,' Ginger said. 'You saw him when he was going to see old Mason about dinner-money. Dinner-money drives Charlie bonkers. He can never get it right. You've got to bring it the first day of every week and you haven't got to want any change. You brought yours?'

I pulled a handful of silver out of my pocket. 'My mother said it would be five shillings.'

Ginger beamed. 'You've got a clever mother, Stew. You give Charlie five bob and you'll be over the first danger. The other one's this. You don't ever call him "Charlie". Not to his face I mean. You call him "Charlie" and he'll bury you. You've got to call him "Charles". What school were you at last?'

'I've never been to school before,' I said.

They gaped at me and somebody said, 'Can you read?'

'Of course I can,' I said. 'My mother and father have been educating me.'

There was a snigger. A little boy on the front row said, 'I'd like to see my dad educating me! He can't do my homework sums now!'

Ginger Evans winked at somebody and then looked again at me, his voice all friendliness, his eyes brilliant with mischief.

'Thought you might have been used to calling teachers "sir",' he said. 'You don't do that with Charlie. He's one of these modern teachers. You call him "Charles" and you stick "Charles" on to everything you say if you don't want him to belt you. "Yes, Charles." That's how you do it. "Thanks very much, Charles." Got it? You do that and you'll be O.K. That right, you lot?'

They were nodding and grinning, and one or two of them were near to bursting.

'You must think everybody's as daft as you are, Evans,' the big boy said.

Ginger didn't hear him. He was too anxious to fill me with information. 'Charlie's got a stick, kid. Keeps it in that cupboard. Most of the teachers don't cane you but Charlie does and Timber Thompson sometimes. Gutsy Collins – he takes P.T. – he uses a slipper. But Charlie's the one to watch. If he uses his stick on you it feels like you've been guillotined. So you give him five bob for your dinners so's he can spend it on whisky at night and you call him "Charles" and you'll be O.K. That's how we do it. Isn't that right, you lot?'

There were frenzied nods and giggles which were strangled when Mr Harris walked into the room. He looked at me.

'You're the new boy. Stewart, is it?'

'Yes, Charles,' I said.

There was a network of tiny purple veins over his cheeks and these were suddenly lost in the redness that flushed into his face. His bottom lip was slightly trembling.

'Somebody told you to say that,' he said and the trembling of his lip became a trembling of his voice. 'Somebody told you to address me in that way. Who was it, Stewart?'

I nodded at Ginger. 'This boy told me your name.'

'When you address me, Stewart,' Mr Harris said, 'call me "sir". "*Sir*", boy.' He went to the cupboard beside the blackboard and without looking at the class he said, 'Come out, Evans!'

Ginger came out, his face brighter than his hair. As he walked past me he punched me in the stomach so hard that I gasped.

'*Snitch!*' I heard somebody whisper.

The boys were glaring at me; all except the big boy next to Ginger. He was smiling a little as he watched me, a shy embarrassed smile.

Mr Harris was holding his cane. It was about three feet long and half an inch thick and it had the cruel curve of a scimitar.

'Your hand, Evans,' he said. 'This is for impertinence.'

Ginger's jaw was set tight and his mouth was a thin straight line. Mr Harris raised the cane and held it high for an immeasurable time while he watched Ginger's unwilling hand like a cat watching a mouse. Then the cane came cutting down across the hand and Ginger jerked and lifted up his right foot.

'The other hand, Evans,' Mr. Harris said. His red face had gone pale and it was damp and shiny. 'This is for trying to get somebody else into trouble.'

Slowly Ginger offered his left hand and I watched the horrifying execution a second time and saw Ginger with his arms across his chest and his hands squeezed under his armpits go back to his desk and hate me with his eyes. I felt that I had shrunk.

'Now you, Stewart,' Mr. Harris said. 'You knew that you were being impertinent so I shall give you one stroke. Hold out your hand.'

I stared at the monster. He was the first teacher I had ever known and he tortured boys into submission. He was something out of a horror-comic and I was not afraid of him.

'No!' I said.

Reginald Maddock

9

All Summer in a Day

'Ready?'

'Ready.'

'Now?'

'Soon.'

'Do the scientists really know? Will it happen today, will it?'

'Look, look; see for yourself!'

The children pressed to each other like so many roses, so many weeds, intermixed, peering out for a look at the hidden sun.

It rained.

It had been raining for seven years, thousands upon thousands of days compounded and filled from one end to the other with rain, with the drum and gush of water, with the sweet crystal fall of showers and the concussion of storms so heavy they were tidal waves come over the islands. A thousand forests had been crushed under the rain and grown up a thousand times to be crushed again. And this was the way life was forever on the planet Venus, and this was the schoolroom of the children of the rocket men and women who had come to a raining world to set up civilisation and live out their lives.

'It's stopping, it's stopping!'

'Yes, yes!'

Margot stood apart from them, from these children who could never remember a time when there wasn't rain and rain and rain. They were all nine years old, and if there had been a day, seven years ago, when the sun came out for an hour and showed its face to the stunned world, they could not recall. Sometimes, at night, she heard them stir, in remembrance, and she knew they were dreaming and remembering gold or a yellow crayon or a coin large enough to buy the world with. She knew that they thought they remembered a warmness, like a blushing in the face, in the body, in the arms and legs and trembling hands. But then they always awoke to the tatting drum, the endless shaking down of clear bead necklaces upon the roof, the walk, the gardens, the forest, and their dreams were gone.

All day yesterday they had read in class, about the sun. About how like a lemon it was, and how hot. And they had written small stories or essays or poems about it:

> I think the sun is a flower,
> That blooms for just one hour.

That was Margot's poem, read in a quiet voice in the still classroom while the rain was falling outside.

'Aw, you didn't write that!' protested one of the boys.

'I did,' said Margot. '*I did.*'

'William!' said the teacher.

But that was yesterday. Now, the rain was slackening, and the children were crushed to the great thick windows.

'Where's teacher?'

'She'll be back.'

'She'd better hurry, we'll miss it!'

They turned on themselves, like a feverish wheel, all tumbling spokes.

Margot stood alone. She was a very frail girl who looked as if she had been lost in the rain for years and the rain had washed out the blue from her eyes and the red from her mouth and the yellow from her hair. She was an old photograph dusted from an album, whitened away, and if she spoke at all her voice would be a ghost. Now she stood, separate, staring at the rain and the loud wet world beyond the huge glass.

'What're *you* looking at?' said William.

Margot said nothing.

'Speak when you're spoken to.' He gave her a shove. But she did not move; rather, she let herself be moved only by him and nothing else.

They edged away from her, they would not look at her. She felt them go away. And this was because she would play no games with them in the echoing tunnels of the underground city. If they tagged her and ran, she stood blinking after them and did not follow. When the class sang songs about happiness and life and games, her lips barely moved. Only when they sang about the sun and the summer did her lips move, as she watched the drenched windows.

And then, of course, the biggest crime of all was that she had come here only five years ago from Earth, and she remembered the sun and the way the sun was and the sky was, when she was four, in Ohio. And they, they had been on Venus all their lives, and they had been only two years old when last the sun came out, and had long since forgotten the colour and heat of it and the way that it really was. But Margot remembered.

'It's like a penny,' she said, once, eyes closed.

'No, it's not!' the children cried.

'It's like a fire,' she said, 'in the stove.'

'You're lying, you don't remember!' cried the children.

But she remembered and stood quietly apart from all of them, and watched the patterning windows. And once, a month ago, she had refused to shower in the school shower rooms, had clutched her hands to her ears and over her head screaming the water mustn't touch her head. So after that, dimly, dimly, she sensed it, she was different and they knew her difference and kept away.

There was talk that her father and mother were taking her back to Earth next year; it seemed vital to her that they do so, though it would mean the loss of thousands of dollars to her family. And so the children hated her for all these reasons, of big and little consequence. They hated her pale snow face, her waiting silence, her thinness and her possible future.

'Get away!' The boy gave her another push. 'What're you waiting for?'

Then, for the first time, she turned and looked at him. And what she was waiting for was in her eyes.

'Well, don't wait around here!' cried the boy, savagely. 'You won't see nothing!'

Her lips moved.

'Nothing!' he cried. 'It was all a joke, wasn't it?' He turned to the other children. 'Nothing's happening today. *Is* it?'

They all blinked at him and then, understanding, laughed and shook their heads. 'Nothing, nothing!'

'Oh, but,' Margot whispered, her eyes were helpless. 'But this is the day, the scientists predict, they say, they *know*, the sun . . .'

'All a joke!' said the boy, and seized her roughly. 'Hey, everyone, let's put her in a closet before teacher comes!'

'No,' said Margot, falling back.

They surged about her, caught her up and bore her, protesting, and then pleading, and then crying, back into a tunnel, a room, a closet, where they slammed and locked the door. They stood looking at the door and saw it tremble from her beating and throwing herself against it. They heard her muffled cries. Then, smiling, they turned and went out and back down the tunnel, just as the teacher arrived.

'Ready, children?' She glanced at her watch.

'Yes!' said everyone.

'Are we all here?'

'Yes!'

The rain slackened still more.

They crowded to the huge door.

The rain stopped.

It was as if, in the midst of a film concerning an avalanche, a tornado, a hurricane, a volcanic eruption, something had, first, gone wrong with the sound apparatus, thus muffling and cutting off all noise, all of the blasts and repercussions and thunders, and then secondly, ripped the film from the projector and inserted in its place a peaceful tropical slide which did not move or tremor. The world ground to a standstill. The silence was so immense and unbelievable that you felt that your ears had been stuffed or you had lost your hearing altogether. The children put their hands to their ears. They stood apart. The door slid back and the smell of the silent, waiting world came in to them.

The sun came out.

It was the colour of flaming bronze and it was very large. And the sky around it was a blazing blue tile colour. And the jungle burned with sunlight as the children released from their spell, rushed out, yelling, into the summertime.

'Now, don't go too far,' called the teacher after them. 'You've only one hour, you know. You wouldn't want to get caught out!'

But they were running and turning their faces up to the sky and feeling the sun on their cheeks like a warm iron; they were taking off their jackets and letting the sun burn their arms.

'Oh, it's better than sun lamps, isn't it?'

'Much, much better!'

They stopped running and stood in the great jungle that covered Venus, that grew and never stopped growing, tumultuously, even as you watched it. It was a nest of octopuses, clustering up great arms of fleshlike weed, wavering, flowering in this brief spring. It was the colour of rubber and ash, this jungle, from many years without sun. It was the colour of stones and white cheeses and ink.

The children lay out, laughing, on the jungle mattress, and heard it sigh and squeak under them, resilient and alive. They ran among the trees, they slipped and fell, they pushed each other, they played hide-and-seek and tag, but most of all they squinted at the sun until tears ran down their faces, they put their hands up at that yellowness and that amazing blueness and they breathed of the fresh air and listened and listened to the silence which suspended in a blessed sea of no sound and no motion. They looked at everything and savoured everything. Then, wildly, like animals escaped from their caves, they ran and ran in shouting circles. They ran for an hour and did not stop running.

And then –

In the midst of their running, one of the girls wailed.

Everyone stopped.

The girl, standing in the open, held out her hand.

'Oh, look, look,' she said, trembling.

They came slowly to look at her opened palm.

In the centre of it, cupped and huge, was a single raindrop.

She began to cry, looking at it.

They glanced quickly at the sky.

'Oh. Oh.'

A few cold drops fell on their noses and their cheeks and their mouths. The sun faded behind a stir of mist. A wind blew cool around them. They turned and started to walk back toward the underground house, their hands at their sides, their smiles vanishing away.

A boom of thunder startled them and like leaves before a new hurricane, they tumbled upon each other and ran. Lightning struck ten miles away, five miles away, a mile, a half mile. The sky darkened into midnight in a flash.

They stood in the doorway of the underground for a moment until it was raining hard. Then they closed the door and heard the gigantic sound of the rain falling in tons and avalanches everywhere and forever.

'Will it be seven more years?'

'Yes. Seven.'

Then one of them gave a little cry.

'Margot!'

'What?'

'She's still in the closet where we locked her.'

'Margot.'

They stood as if someone had driven them, like so many stakes, into the floor. They looked at each other and then looked away. They glanced out at the world that was raining now and raining and raining steadily. They could not meet each other's glances. Their faces were solemn and pale. They looked at their hands and feet, their faces down.

'Margot.'

One of the girls said, 'Well . . . ?'

No one moved.

'Go on,' whispered the girl.

They walked slowly down the hall in the sound of cold rain. They turned through the doorway to the room, in the sound of the storm and thunder, lightning on their faces, blue and terrible. They walked over to the closet door slowly and stood by it.

Behind the closet door was only silence.

They unlocked the door, even more slowly, and let Margot out.

Ray Bradbury

Streemin

Im in the botom streme
Which meens Im not brigth
dont like reading
cant hardly write

but all these divishns
arnt reely fair
look at the cemtery
no streemin there

Roger McGough

Rythm

They dunno how it is. I smack a ball
right through the goals. But they dunno how the words
get muddled in my head, get tired somehow.
I look through the window, see. And there's a wall
I'd kick the ball against, just smack and smack.
Old Jerry he can't play, he don't know how,
not now at any rate. He's too flicking small.
See him in shorts, out in the crazy black.
Rythm, he says,and ryme. See him at back.
He don't know nuthing about Law. He'd fall
flat on his face, just like a big sack,
when you're going down the wing, the wind behind you
and crossing into the goalmouth and they're roaring
the whole great crowd. They're up on their feet cheering.
The ball's at your feet and there it goes, just crack.
Old Jerry dives – the wrong way. And they're jearing
and I run to the centre and old Bash
jumps up and down, and I feel great, and wearing
my gold and purpel strip, fresh from the wash.

Iain Crichton Smith

11

Lord of the Flies

'What's your name?'

'Ralph.'

The fat boy waited to be asked his name in turn but this proffer of acquaintance was not made; the fair boy called Ralph smiled vaguely, stood up, and began to make his way once more towards the lagoon. The fat boy hung steadily at his shoulder.

'I expect there's a lot more of us scattered about. You haven't seen any others have you?'

Ralph shook his head and increased his speed. Then he tripped over a branch and came down with a crash.

The fat boy stood by him, breathing hard.

'My auntie told me not to run,' he explained, 'on account of my asthma.'

'Ass-mar?'

'That's right. Can't catch me breath. I was the only boy in our school what had asthma,' said the fat boy with a touch of pride. 'And I've been wearing specs since I was three.'

He took off his glasses and held them out to Ralph, blinking and smiling, and then started to wipe them against his grubby wind-breaker. An expression of pain and inward concentration altered the pale contours of his face. He smeared the sweat from his cheeks and quickly adjusted the spectacles on his nose.

'Them fruit.'

He glanced round the scar.

'Them fruit,' he said, 'I expect —'

He put on his glasses, waded away from Ralph, and crouched down among the tangled foliage.

'I'll be out again in just a minute —'

Ralph disentangled himself cautiously and stole away through the branches. In a few seconds the fat boy's grunts were behind him and he was hurrying towards the screen that still lay between him and the lagoon. He climbed over a broken trunk and was out of the jungle.

He jumped down from the terrace. The sand was thick over his black shoes and the heat hit him. He became conscious of the weight of clothes, kicked his shoes off fiercely and ripped off each stocking with its elastic garter in a single movement. Then he leapt back on the terrace, pulled off his shirt, and stood there among the skull-like coco-nuts with green shadows from the palms and the forest sliding over his skin. He undid the snake-clasp of his belt, lugged off his shorts and pants, and stood there naked, looking at the dazzling beach and the water.

He was old enough, twelve years and a few months, to have lost the prominent tummy of childhood; and not yet old enough for adolescence to have made him awkward. You could see now that he might make a boxer, as far as width and heaviness of shoulders went, but there was a mildness about his mouth and eyes that proclaimed no devil. He patted the palm trunk softly; and, forced at last to believe in the reality of the island, laughed delightedly again and stood on his head. He turned neatly on to his feet, jumped down to the beach, knelt and swept a double armful of sand into a pile against his chest. Then he sat back and looked at the water with bright, excited eyes.

'Ralph —'

The fat boy lowered himself over the terrace and sat down carefully, using the edge as a seat.

'I'm sorry I been such a time. Them fruit —'

He wiped his glasses and adjusted them on his button nose. The frame had made a deep, pink 'V' on the bridge. He looked critically at Ralph's golden body and then down at his own clothes. He laid a hand on the end of a zipper that extended down his chest.

'My auntie —'

Then he opened the zipper with decision and pulled the whole wind-breaker over his head.

'There!'

Ralph looked at him side-long and said nothing.

'I expect we'll want to know all their names,' said the fat boy, 'and make a list. We ought to have a meeting.'

Ralph did not take the hint so the fat boy was forced to continue.

'I don't care what they call me,' he said confidentially, 'so long as they don't call me what they used to call me at school.'

Ralph was faintly interested.

'What was that?'

The fat boy glanced over his shoulder, then leaned towards Ralph.

He whispered.

'They used to call me "Piggy".'

Ralph shrieked with laughter. He jumped up.

'Piggy! Piggy!'

'Ralph – please!'

Piggy clasped his hands in apprehension.

'I said I didn't want – '

'Piggy! Piggy!'

Ralph danced out into the hot air of the beach and then returned as a fighter-plane, with wings swept back, and machine-gunned Piggy.

'Sche – aa – ow!'

He dived in the sand at Piggy's feet and lay there laughing.

'Piggy!'

Piggy grinned reluctantly, pleased despite himself at even this much recognition.

'So long as you don't tell the others – '

William Golding

12

The Advertisement

Geordie went straight out of the kitchen and up the rickety steps to his own room. It was small, in below the roof of the cottage, and there was just space for his bed and the dresser with his hairbrush on it. He took a look at himself in the mirror. Somehow you'd expect when you felt so bad that it would show in your face: but there was no difference. It was the same awful red face and the same carroty hair. That was wee Geordie in the mirror, wee to Jean, wee to the boys at the school, wee to Dad and Mum. Too wee to be any use for anything, too wee to be as good as a lassie in a climb.

There were some old magazines in the corner of the room. Geordie had read them all before, for he was a great reader even if reading took time because he was slow in his thoughts as well as in his growing. But he needed something to take his mind off his troubles, so he fetched a couple of mags and took off his boots for fear Mum would come up and catch him with them on the bed and he lay on his back and began to read the old stuff again. There were some adventure stories and some about love. He never bothered with the love ones. Love was daft. But he liked fine to read adventure.

His favourite was about a boy asleep in bed at night and he wakes up sudden and hears noises in the house, so he ups and tiptoes to the door not making any creak on the boards. 'Please turn to Page 46,' it said when the story was just getting exciting. Geordie knew fine what was coming, but it still had him gripped every time he read it, so he flipped over fast to page 46 hardly able to wait for the boy to crack the burglar over the head and be the hero of the village.

Here was page 46 and . . . But Geordie stopped. He was seeing something he'd never noticed any of the other times. It stood up on the printed page and smacked him in the eye. He looked away to go on reading the story, and looked back again. That was how it smacked him, and him being the boy in the dark house not knowing what was round the corner, and then forgetting all that quite sudden.

It was an advertisement, tucked up there in the corner, an advert with two small pictures. Geordie read it through once.

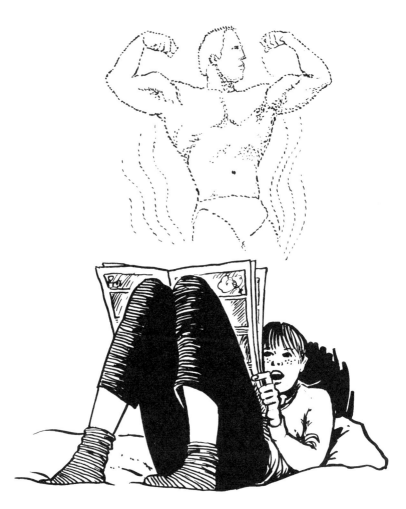

Then he read it again. This is what he read:

Are you undersized? Do people ignore you? No need for despair! Grow big the Samson way! Write for my only unique course in physical culture. You can be strong! You can be tall! Balanced development is my motto. World-wide testimonials. For proof of success see untouched photographs below.

Send ten shillings only for complete course in plain wrapper. Your problems will receive personal attention of the great Henry Samson, six foot four and the world's strongest man.

Write P.O. Box 689, Wadsworth, London, N.10. Satisfaction guaranteed.

Geordie suddenly felt very tired. He didn't know why that should happen to him; a ten-mile walk up the glen was nothing on a Saturday; nothing ever made him tired, even if he was small. Perhaps it was just the great idea striking him. Yes, it must be that. He closed his eyes for a minute, lying quite slack, seeing wonderful pictures of him big and strong. Then he opened his eyes again to read the advert. The man was a wee stoopy thing *before*, but he had a chest like a barrel on him *after*, and tall.

Ten bob was a big price. It was a huge price; and how would you know it wasn't just a have-on? Them English with their fancy ways. What Dad said came into his mind – 'it's jest blether blether[1] wi' the Sassenachs[2], full o' fancy capers. I've no time for them.'

But he looked again. There was something about it that wasn't just English blether: 'World-wide testimonials, before and after, six foot four, satisfaction guaranteed.'

No, it read like it was true. Ten bob was a lot, but he'd earned more than that at the potato-picking last year. Still, that was last year and he didn't have ten bob now.

Geordie went over to the dresser and took his money-box out of the drawer. He undid the sticky tape and opened the box, knowing near enough what was there, but not knowing exactly. He counted it up. Seven shillings and eightpence it came to. The eightpence would do the postal order and the stamp. That left three bob to get.

Generally Geordie took a long time to decide things; but not now. He'd made up his mind already what he was to do, and he knew that the Samson course, English or no, was a right good bargain. He was sure of it. What was ten bob if you could be as big as Henry Samson?

David Walker

[1]blether: talk.
[2]Sassenachs: English.

'I Want to be England Manager': Peter Shilton Speaks

It is not difficult to understand why Peter Shilton's book is called *The Magnificent Obsession*.

When only nine years old and playing for his primary school, he would go home after games and draw diagrams of situations that had arisen in the matches so that he could improve his angles. This way, he thought he would be able to avoid making the same mistake again.

As a young lad, he would hang from a bar to make his arms longer; and his parents would help him by pulling on his legs. The result is that Shilton's arms are now two inches longer than would be normal.

For Shilton, performing miracles is something he expects of himself, not just something he hopes for.

'It's never been enough for me to be just a solid, reliable goalkeeper,' he says. 'They're big assets but you want to be able to perform a few miracles from time to time. I hate it when people say I had no chance with a goal. Obviously it's right in some cases, but I've seen 'keepers let in so-called "wonder goals" which I know they could have saved had they been good enough.

'About ten times a season I'll make a save which will stem, not just from my training, but from something I've been born with. I'll surprise myself and when that happens, I get a feeling of elation as opposed to satisfaction.

'I'm not superhuman, but when I'm really on song I do sense opponents thinking "How the hell are we going to beat him?"'

Shilton is now 32 and has 35 caps spread over 12 years. Apart from wanting to be recognised as the world's top goalkeeper, Shilton has also set his sights on becoming manager of England. He is a single-minded man who has set himself the most incredible high standards, a man who is unwilling to compromise in any way.

'It's an annoying part of me – something inside me which won't tolerate second best. I don't want people to expect unbelievable things from me, but at the same time I expect unbelievable things of myself.'

Adapted from *Shoot*, April 1982

Mrs O'Neill

(A TALE OF UNREQUITED LOVE)

Every evening
Before she went to bed
Mrs O'Neill said
Goodnight
To that nice announcer
On her small TV
Because she was eighty
And very much alone.

And when she died
He never even went
To her funeral.

Richard Hill

15

In and Out of the Box

Some people seem to think we are exalted beings. One day I answered the office telephone and a rather blah male voice at the other end was asking, 'Is that Mr Dougall's private secretary?' It was a retired Naval Commander asking me to open a fête or something. As a matter of fact, we don't have secretaries, let alone a private one. So, if a viewer or listener writes in, he or she really does get a personal reply. This, it seems to me, is an important part of the job. The letters are incidentally a startling indication of the numbers of lonely people in our society today. For them, especially, the News-reader appearing in their homes night after night over the years becomes, it would seem, almost a trusted friend. He regularly brings news and information, if not always good tidings. His dress and appearance are usually neat and mostly inoffensive. He never answers back, doesn't even smell, and smiles when he says good night. All that, judging by the letters, can add up to quite an important relationship. It does not seem to be confined to any age group, as I get many letters from school children (heaven knows they can be lonely too); also from teenagers, and frequently even from married couples.

Can it be that change of all kinds is so frequent and endemic in our life today that a television Newsreader can become a reliable symbol of permanence and continuity? After all, under present conditions, the family doctor, as we used to know him, has almost ceased to exist. The local vicar doesn't quite fill the role he used to either, and in many cases, even the small shopkeeper has given way to an impersonal supermarket. In these conditions, perhaps it is not so surprising that lonely people will look even to an electronic image for reassurance. Some letters make me feel very humble, indeed almost all of them make me feel my job is, in a sense, a privilege. For example, when someone writes to say how much I have helped them at a difficult time in their life, I am inclined to be incredulous. How can you help a person by just giving out the News on television? But this has happened so many times I can only think it is because they can at least rely on my being there.

Letters often come from people when they move house or go on holiday. They say how pleased they were when they reached the new, unfamiliar surroundings to find I was on the box there too. Some of the most interesting letters of this kind have come from as far away as Australia when, to inaugurate the opening of the Pacific Satellite in 1970, a fifteen-minute News programme read by me was televised live from Television Centre in London across the length and breadth of Australia.

But there is no doubt that of all the thousands of letters I've received from viewers in the past fifteen years or so my favourite came from an old lady who lived somewhere in Hertfordshire. I think I ought to have it framed. She wrote to me, in a spidery hand, to say that she was a little deaf, so she did like to sit right close up to her machine, as she called it, when I was giving the News. But, if this put me off in any way, she would quite understand and move further back. Really, the height of consideration. Recently at a function, a dear old lady caused some raised eyebrows. She came up to me confidingly and then piped up at the top of her voice: 'There's one thing about you Mr Dougall – you're the nicest man I know to go to bed with!' She then explained that she had recently installed a TV set in her bedroom.

It is evident too, that a lot of people seem to think I can see them. There was a letter from Scotland, which came from a crofter's cottage in the Highlands. They were living in pretty close quarters there and a member of the family wrote to say that Grannie was preparing for bed when the News was switched on. They were tickled to find that Grannie got very upset and kept tugging her gown across her chest, as she said, 'I dinna want him tae see me like this!' Another letter, written to a Sunday paper, came from a good lady who used to take her portable television set with her when she was having a bath! Everything was going swimmingly until I came on to give the News. At that point, she let out a yell, scrambled out of the bath, rushed to the set and covered it with a towel! Then, I was told of an old-age pensioner in Harrogate. Every time she drew her pension, it seems, she would come home and hide it in a tobacco jar on the mantelpiece. But, before doing so, she took great care to make sure the television set was well and truly covered up, just in case I was looking.

Robert Dougall

16

The Boy with the Transistor Radio

We see a view through the window of archetypal suburban England, the England of the advertisers, heavy with blossom and perfectly in order. Then we hear FLOAT

FLOAT: Float Jones on 209. It's music, music everyday. Music to make you feel good, music to make you feel alive. Get into the clouds with this one.

He fades in the guitar solo from 'Feel the Benefit, Part 3' (10cc). We hear TERRY's *dad from downstairs.*

MR DAVIES *(Calling)*: Terry ... Terry ...

Terry's bedroom

TERRY *is looking out of the window. We are now shown reality, from* TERRY's *point of view.*

TERRY *(Lowering the volume of the radio)*: What?

MR DAVIES: Up!

TERRY: All right. *(He turns the radio up)*

MRS DAVIES *(Calling)*: Terry ... Terry ...

TERRY *(To himself)*: Tch ... *(Calls)* What?

MRS DAVIES *(Calling from the foot of the stairs)*: We're off. see y' tonight. Listen, son ... make sure y' in early. Y' dad's gonna find out about gettin' y' in at his place ... in the warehouse ... *(Pause)* Did you hear me, Terry?

TERRY: Yeh. *(Turns up the radio)*

MRS DAVIES *(Going)*: Tarar.

TERRY *(To himself)*: Warehouse! I'm not gonna work in a warehouse, am I, Float? I'm gonna do something like you. I'm gonna do somethin' good, somethin' that makes y' feel as good as the music does.

He begins to mime playing a guitar to music. He sees his battered acoustic, takes it and pretends to play it. Then he ventures a note. It clashes with the music from the radio. It's obvious that he can't play. He puts it down again and mimes playing to the music from the radio.

The street

Kids are making their way to school and there are long bus queues. TERRY *is looking through some railings at a factory warehouse. It could be confused with a prison.* TERRY *pulls himself away and moves on. He takes a lead from his pocket and plugs it into his ear. We hear the radio.*

FLOAT: It's 209 telling you it's good to be alive. Float Jones looking after you, guaranteeing you a good day all the way with 209. the fabulous frequency, the wonderful waveband. ... Yes!

A school hall

The HEADMASTER *is talking to the gathering.*

HEADMASTER: And we're getting close to that time of the year when some of you will be leaving us to take jobs. The lucky ones. Yes, lucky. Because in this day and age it isn't easy to get a job, as we all know from the newspapers and television, don't we — you!

BOY *(Startled)*: Yes, sir!

HEADMASTER: Yes. Those of us who have jobs today have to be grateful.

He surveys the mass of faces before him. We see it from his point of view and locate TERRY *who is staring, apparently attentively up at him.*

Some of us are in for a shock as well. I'll tell you why; you lads who have resented coming to school, you girls who have complained year in year out about disliking school, you'll change your attitude after you've been out in the world for a couple of years because, believe me, it's not all milk and honey out there, you know. It's not all that the pop magazines and television and the advertisers would have you believe. No. And I'll tell you something — when you walk in through the school gates for the first time you're coming in for eleven, maybe twelve years. But most of you, when you walk into your working life, you're going in for forty years. Yes. Forty years ... *(He nods)*

Now we see the HEADMASTER *from* TERRY's *point of view and as we hear the guitar solo from 'Feel the Benefit'.* TERRY *has his earplug in again. At the end of the song, we hear* FLOAT's *voice.*

FLOAT: It's summertime. Yes ... it's summertime on 209 and the livin' sure is easy.

We see the platform from TERRY's *point of view. In* TERRY's *imagination, the* HEADMASTER *has been replaced by* FLOAT.

FLOAT: You feel a little down, you feel a little blue ... Listen to Float, he'll tell you what to do. Listen to the music on 209 make ya better, make ya feel fine ... Just do what ya wanna do ...

A classroom

Kids are waiting for a teacher. TERRY *is sitting at the back, leaning back on his chair, looking out of window. The* TEACHER *enters.*

TEACHER: Mornin'.

GIRL 1: Hia, sir.

BOY 1: All right, sir.

BRIAN: What happened to your team last night then, sir?

TEACHER: What d' y' mean, 'What happened?' What happened was that we had a referee who'd left his contact lenses out. *(Good natured laughter and derision from the class)* OK, let's have a bit of hush ... Hey!

The class quietens.

GIRL 1: Ah'ey ... we're not doin' any work, are we, sir?

BOY 1: There's no point.

KATHY: We're leavin' next week.

TEACHER: Have you got a job yet, Kath?

KATHY: Yes, sir. Our Maureen's got me fixed up at her place — y' know, Clifford's Biscuits.

TEACHER: Good, good. What will you be doing?

During the following dialogue TERRY *becomes bored. He takes out his transistor lead and surreptitiously plugs it in.*

KATHY: Sir, at first I'll be sortin' the biscuits, y'know, the ones that get broke ...

GIRL 1: They let y' buy them cheap, y' know, the broken ones.

KATHY: I know. But, sir, y'know, later on, when I've got used to the job. I'll have me own machine an' I'll be makin' proper biscuits then.

We hear the song. 'Wonderful World', TERRY is looking out of the window. The school dissolves to a shot of a group of bright young people sitting about on the thick grass in the gardens of a public school. We return to the classroom.

TEACHER: ... That's great, Brian. You start next week?

BRIAN: Yes, sir.

TEACHER: Good. (*Turns to* TERRY) Terry ... what about you?

TERRY is unaware that he is being addressed. We hear music again.

TEACHER: Have you got a job, Terry?

TERRY stares at him but makes no effort to answer. The TEACHER is puzzled

TEACHER: Terry ... Terry!

The kids in the class turn and look at him and laugh. BRIAN, leaning across, unseen by TERRY, pulls the lead from his ear. TERRY is startled, sheepish.

TEACHER (*To class*): All right, all right ... Calm down ...

KATHY: He's always listenin' to that radio, sir.

TEACHER: Is he? Well, Terry, if I could just interrupt for a minute or two ... I was askin' if you had a job yet.

TERRY shrugs

KATHY: His Dad's gettin' him a job in their place, sir, in the warehouse.

TERRY: No, he's not.

KATHY: Yes, he is. Your mam told me mother an' she told me.

TERRY: Y' don't wanna listen to me mother. What does she know about it?

KATHY: That's what she said.

TERRY: Yeh, but she doesn't realize. Just 'cos she goes out every day doin' a job that she hates she thinks I'm gonna have to do the same. But I'm not gonna work in a ware-house.

TEACHER: Well, what are you going to do, Terry?

TERRY: Sir, I'll have a proper job, somethin' dead smart that I enjoy doin'. I'm gettin' a job with travel prospects an' a car. An' when I grow up I'll have a wife who's dead smart with proper, nice kids an' a house in the country an', y'know ... all that!

BOY 1: The only house you'll see in the country is the looney house.

Laughter

TERRY: You're the one who should be in a looney house ...

TEACHER: Ah ah ah ... Now! Terry ... listen, how do you plan to achieve all this?

TERRY: What d' y' mean, sir? It just comes to y', doesn't it?

BRIAN: But y' have to work for it, soft lad.

TERRY: Well ... I'm gonna work. But I'm not takin' the sort of job you've got, Lino. I'm not clockin' in for the rest of me life. ...

BRIAN: Shut it, you ... soft ...

TEACHER: Terry! Exactly what sort of job do you have in mind for yourself?

TERRY: Sir, somethin' in the music business.

TEACHER: The music business?

BRIAN: Goin' on the stage, are y' Terry lad?

BOY 2: They wouldn't let him on the landing stage.

BRIAN: Sir, don't believe him, he's lyin'.

BOY 1: He's a looney, Sir.

KATHY: Sir, he's not got a job in the music business. he's soft.

TEACHER: Terry? Well?

TERRY: Well, what ... I'm not talkin' to them, they're just jealous.

TEACHER: Well, Terry. You've got to admit that this future you've got mapped out ... it does seem a bit impressive. I mean the music business isn't one you just walk into, is it?

TERRY: No.

BRIAN: See. ... Don't believe him, sir ...

TERRY (*Pause*): But I know someone who's gonna get me fixed up.

KIDS: Who? Who is it ...? What's his name?

TERRY: Never you mind.

KIDS (*Derision*): Ah ...

TERRY: Sir ... I know someone in the music business. ... He's a good friend ... a really good friend.

BRIAN: What's his name?

TERRY He's great, sir. Sir, I listen to him cos, cos the things he tells me about, y'know, about, like livin' they're the best things I've ever heard. ...

TEACHER: Well, I'm glad you've been listenin' to someone, because in the five years you've been in this school I don't

think you've listened to any of the staff, have you?

TERRY: No, sir.

TEACHER: Well Terry ... all this good living that you're telling us about ... you'd stand a much better chance of achievin' it if you had listened to us.

TERRY: But, sir, all you and the other teachers, all you ever told us to do was study, an' work hard an' try our best an' take what we get. An' like sometimes I've tried to do that ...

KATHY: He's never tried to work hard, sir ...

TERRY: Yes I have ... I've tried. ... You don't know about it, but I have. ... An' it's no good, cos it's too hard. ... There's too much against y'. Like if I'd started doin' that when I first come to school, when I was a little kid, I'd be OK. But I didn't. An' it's too late now. I'll never get what I want by just studyin' an' workin' hard. It's just dead lucky for me that I've got a friend like Float.

KIDS (*Stunned*): Who?

TERRY: Float.

BRIAN: Float Jones?

TERRY: Yeh.

The class shout protests, claiming that TERRY *doesn't know him.*

TEACHER (*Getting the class quiet*): Look ... who ...?

KATHY: Float Jones. ... He's a DJ, sir....

BOY 1: On the radio....

BOY 2: How could he know Float Jones, sir? He comes from a different world....

TEACHER: Do you know him, Terry?

TERRY: Sir, he's a good friend.

The TEACHER *nods, knowing what* TERRY *means.* TERRY, *turning, looks out of the window.*

The school grounds

We hear the guitar solo from 'Feel the Benefit'. TERRY *is lying on the grass. The* TEACHER *appears and looks down at* TERRY. *He is mouthing something.* TERRY *removes the earplug.*

TEACHER: Can I have a word with you, Terry?

TERRY (*As if to stand*): Yes, sir.

TEACHER: No, it's all right ... stay there ... (*Sits alongside* TERRY)

TERRY (*Looking at him*): What's up, sir?

TEACHER: Listen, Terry, don't you think that you listen to that thing a bit too much.

TERRY: Why, sir?

TEACHER: Well, I mean, there are other things in life.

TERRY: I know, sir.

TEACHER: Well?

TERRY (*Puzzled*): Well what? (*Pause*) Sir, sir, I'd rather listen to me radio....

TEACHER: Yes, but ... but, I mean, you don't want to start believing in it.

TERRY: Sir, why not?

TEACHER: Well it's not ... I mean ... it's not real, is it? It's not life.

TERRY: It is to me.

TEACHER (*Looking at him*): Is it?

TERRY: Sir, I'd rather listen to a trannie any day than have to think about depressin' things.

TEACHER: Which depressing things?

TERRY: You know, sir.

TEACHER: I don't. ... You tell me ...

TERRY: You know ... depressin'. Like, y' know ... livin' round here. It's hardly paradise, is it?

TEACHER (*Pause*): There are worse places.

TERRY: I know, but I live *here*.

The TEACHER *looks at him.* TERRY *suddenly smiles.*

TERRY: Sir, I don't half feel sorry for you.

TEACHER (*Smiling, puzzled*): Why?

TERRY: Well, it's like ... you've been tryin' to teach us lot for the last five years, haven't y'?. An', like most of us, we're gonna walk out them gates as thick as when we come in, aren't we?

TEACHER: Come on ... you've learnt somethin' since you've been here....

TERRY: Oh, yeh. But I mean, there's none of us gonna light up the world as far as brains are concerned. But just think, sir, just think that if you'd been a DJ for the last five years — just think how many people would have listened to y' then, an' they would have listened properly. No talkin' at the back or missin' lessons then. Know what I mean, sir?

TEACHER: Well ... erm ... er, yes ... I think so. ...

TERRY: Yeh.

TEACHER: Terry ... listen ... look.... Radios, the music you listen to, the disc jockeys and the advertising — that sort of thing ... you've got to realize that all that sort of thing is a reflection of a world that is not necessarily accurate. Just because you listen to the radio a lot, Terry, it doesn't mean that you'll live your life in paradise. (*Pause*) I mean, these fellows on the radio station who are telling you that everything's fine, everything's easy and uncomplicated — well, you're not ... you're not meant to believe it.

TERRY (*Emphatic*): You are, y' know , sir.

TEACHER (*Slightly impatient*): Look, lad ... I'm trying to be realistic and make you see sense. I mean ... the special jobs ... the super jobs, there's only a very few of those going. Most of us have to put up with the ordinary day-to-day jobs — doing the best we can. We might want more; but we've got to be prepared for the fact that we mightn't get it. Understand?

TERRY *nods and plugs in his ear-piece.*

TEACHER: I mean, the DJs might suggest that you're in Seventh Heaven but you're not ... none of us are. Just because there's a picture of life up on a street poster doesn't mean to say that it's yours for the asking. (*The school bell rings*) Well ... come on ... I suppose we'd better get in. ... Come on now. ... (*He sees some boys at the far end of the field. He shouts*) Come on, you lads ... look sharp. ...

The TEACHER *walks towards the school building. We hear the final bars of 'Wonderful World' as we watch the stragglers make their way into the school building.* TERRY *lies back on the grass. At the end of the song* FLOAT*'s voice is heard.*

FLOAT: Ah yes ... I said to myself ... what a wonderful world. Right now, just stop whatever you're doing, open your eyes and have a look at that great big wonderful world. (*We look, as instructed by* FLOAT. *We see nothing sensational, just the facts, the school and the surrounding streets*) It's a beautiful day on 209, the sun's shining and everything's fine; England ... you're beautiful — isn't she beautiful ...? Yes. Good to have you along. I'm feeling good, you're feeling good, which adds up to the fact that we're all feeling good ... and that's good. ...

Warning

When I am an old woman I shall wear purple
With a red hat which doesn't go, and doesn't suit me,
And I shall spend my pension on brandy and summer gloves
And satin sandals, and say we've no money for butter.
I shall sit down on the pavement when I'm tired
And gobble up samples in shops and press alarm bells
And run my stick along the public railings
And make up for the sobriety of my youth.
I shall go out in my slippers in the rain
And pick the flowers in other people's gardens
And learn to spit.

You can wear terrible shirts and grow more fat
And eat three pounds of sausages at a go
Or only bread and pickle for a week
And hoard pens and pencils and beermats and things in boxes.

But now we must have clothes that keep us dry
And pay the rent and not swear in the street
And set a good example for the children.
We must have friends to dinner and read the papers.

But maybe I ought to practise a little now?
So people who know me are not too shocked and surprised
When suddenly I am old and start to wear purple.

Jenny Joseph

Note for the Future

When I get old
don't dress me in
frayed jackets
and too-short trousers
and send me out
to sit around bowling greens
in summer.
Don't give me just enough
to exist on and expect me
to like passing
the winter days
in the reading room
of the local library, waiting
my turn to read
last night's local paper.
Shoot me!
Find a reason, any reason,
say I'm a trouble maker,
or can't take care of myself
and live in a dirty room.
If you're afraid
of justifying my execution
on those terms,
tell everyone I leer
at little girls, and then
shoot me!
I don't care why you do it,
but do it,
and don't leave me
to walk to corner-shops
counting my coppers,
or give me a pass to travel cheap
at certain times, like a leper.

Don't send me to a home
to sit and talk
about the weather.
I don't want free tours,
half-price afternoon film-shows,
and friendly visitors.
If I can't live in independence
get me when I'm sixty-five, and
shoot me, you bastards, shoot me!

Jim Burns

19

Skyscraper Wean[1]

I'm a skyscraper wean; I live on the nineteenth flair[2],
But I'm no' gaun[3] oot tae play ony mair,
'Cause since we moved tae Castlemilk, I'm wastin' away
'Cause I'm gettin' wan[4] meal less every day:

Chorus
Oh ye cannae fling pieces[5] oot a twenty storey flat,
Seven hundred hungry weans'll testify to that.
If it's butter, cheese or jeely, if the breid is plain or pan[6],
The odds against it reaching earth are ninety-nine tae wan.

On the first day ma maw[7] flung oot a daud o' Hovis broon[8];
It came skytin[9] oot the windae and went up insteid o' doon.
Noo every twenty-seven hoors it comes back intae sight
'Cause ma piece went intae orbit and became a satellite.

On the second day ma maw flung me a piece oot wance again.
It went and hut[10] the pilot in a fast low-flying plane.
He scraped it aff his goggles, shouting through the intercom,
'The Clydeside Reds[11] huv goat[12] me wi' a breid-an-jeely
bomb.'

On the third day ma maw thought she would try another throw.
The Salvation Army band was staunin[13] doon below.
'Onward, Christian Soldiers' was the piece they should've
    played
But the oompah man[14] was playing a piece an' marmalade.

We've wrote away to Oxfam to try an' get some aid,
An' a' the weans in Castlemilk have formed a 'piece brigade.'
We're gonnae[15] march to George's Square[16] demanding civil
    rights
Like, nae mair hooses ower piece-flinging height.

Adam McNaughtan

[1]wean: young child.
[2]flair: floor, storey.
[3]gaun: going.
[4]wan: one.
[5]pieces: sandwiches, usually with jam ('jeely').
[6]plain or pan: two different types of bread.
[7]maw: mother.
[8]daud o' Hovis broon: chunk of brown Hovis bread.
[9]skytin': flying.
[10]hut: hit.
[11]Clydeside Reds: a socialist movement during the First World War which nearly led to overt rebellion on Clydeside.
[12]huv goat: have got.
[13]staunin': standing.
[14]oompah man: euphonium player.
[15]gonnae: going to.
[16]George's Square: central square in Glasgow where the city chambers are located.

Back Buchanan Street

A fellow from the Corpie
Just out of planning school
Has told us that we've got to go
Right out of Liverpool.
They're sending us to Kirby
To Skelmersdale and Speke
But we want to stay
Where we used to play
In Back Buchanan Street.

Chorus

Don't want to go to Kirby
Don't want to go to Speke
Don't want to go
From all I know
In Back Buchanan Street.

I'll miss the foghorns on the river
And the old pier head
And slipping up the jiggers[1]
When we're rolling home to bed.
There's lots of other little things
Like putting out the cat
But there's no back door
On the fourteenth floor
Of a Unit Camus flat.

I'll miss the pub around the corner
And the parlour painted red
Like I miss the green goddesses[2]
And the Overhead.
From Walton to the Dingle
You'll hear the same old cry
Stop messing round with Liverpool
At least until we die.

I'll miss the Mary-Ellens[3]
And me dad'll miss the docks
And me gran'll miss the wash-house
Where she washed me grandad's socks.
They've pulled down Paddy's Market
Where me mam once had a stall
And soon their picks and shovels
Will be through our backyard wall.

G. and H. Dyson

[1]jiggers: back alleys.
[2]green goddesses: tram cars.
[3]Mary-Ellens: female market stall-holders.

20

On Saturday Afternoon

I once saw a bloke try to kill himself. I'll never forget the day because I was sitting in the house one Saturday afternoon, feeling black and fed-up because everybody in the family had gone to the pictures, except me who'd for some reason been left out of it. 'Course, I didn't know then that I would soon see something you can never see in the same way on the pictures, a real bloke stringing himself up. I was only a kid at the time, so you can imagine how much I enjoyed it.

I've never known a family to look as black as our family when they're fed-up. I've seen the old man with his face so dark and full of murder because he ain't got no fags or was having to use saccharine to sweeten his tea, or even for nothing at all, that I've backed out of the house in case he got up from his fireside chair and came for me. He just sits, almost on top of the fire, his oil-stained Sunday-joint maulers opened out in front of him and facing inwards to each other, his thick shoulders scrunched forward, and his dark brown eyes staring into the fire. Now and again he'd say a dirty word, for no reason at all, the worst word you can think of, and when he starts saying this you know it's time to clear out. If mam's in it gets worse than ever, because she says sharp to him: 'What are yo' looking so bleddy black for?' as if it might be because of something she's done, and before you know what's happening he's tipped up a tableful of pots and mam's gone out of the house crying. Dad hunches back over the fire and goes on swearing. All because of a packet of fags.

I once saw him broodier than I'd ever seen him, so that I thought he'd gone crackers in a quiet sort of way — until a fly flew to within a yard of him. Then his hand shot out, got it, and slung it crippled into the roaring fire. After that he cheered up a bit and mashed some tea.

Well, that's where the rest of us get our black looks from. It stands to reason we'd have them with a dad who carries on like that, don't it? Black looks run in the family. Some families have them and some don't. Our family has them right enough, and that's certain, so when we're fed-up we're really fed-up. Nobody knows why we get as fed-up as we do or why it gives us these black looks when we are. Some people get fed-up and don't look bad at all: they seem happy in a funny sort of way, as if they've just been set free from clink after being in there for something they didn't do, or come out of the pictures after sitting plugged for eight hours at a bad film, or just missed a bus they ran half a mile for and seen it was the wrong one just after they'd stopped running — but in our family it's murder for the others if one of us is fed-up. I've asked myself lots of times what it is, but I can never get any sort of answer even if I sit and think for hours, which I must admit I don't do, though it looks good when I say I do. But I sit and think for long enough, until mam says to me, at seeing me scrunched up over the fire like dad: 'What are yo' looking so black for?' So I've just got to stop thinking about it in case I get really black and fed-up and go the same way as dad, tipping up a tableful of pots and all.

Mostly I suppose there's nothing to look so black for: though it's nobody's fault and you can't blame anyone for looking black because I'm sure it's summat in the blood. But on this Saturday afternoon I was looking so black that when dad came in from the bookie's he said to me: 'What's up wi' yo'?'

'I feel badly,' I fibbed. He'd have had a fit if I'd said I was only black because I hadn't gone to the pictures.

'Well have a wash,' he told me.

'I don't want a wash,' I said, and that was a fact.

'Well, get outside and get some fresh air then,' he shouted.

I did as I was told, double-quick, because if ever dad goes as far as to tell me to get some fresh air I know it's time to get away from him. But outside the air wasn't so fresh, what with that bloody great bike factory bashing away at the yard-end. I didn't know where to go, so I walked up the yard a bit and sat down near somebody's back gate.

Then I saw this bloke who hadn't lived long in our yard. He was tall and thin and had a face like a parson except that he wore a flat cap and had a moustache that drooped, and looked as though he hadn't had a square meal for a year. I didn't think much o' this at the time: but I remember that as he turned in by the yard-end one of the nosy gossiping women who stood there every minute of the day except when she trudged to the pawnshop with her husband's bike or best suit, shouted to him: 'What's that rope for, mate?'

He called back: 'It's to 'ang messen[1] wi', missis,' and she

[1] messen: myself

crackled at this bloody good joke so loud and long you'd think
she never heard such a good 'un, though the next day she
crackled on the other side of her fat face.

He walked by me puffing a fag and carrying his coil of
brand-new rope, and he had to step over me to get past. His
boot nearly took my shoulder off, and when I told him to
watch where he was going I don't think he heard me because
he didn't even look round. Hardly anybody was about. All the
kids were still at the pictures, and most of their mams and
dads were downtown doing the shopping.

The bloke walked down the yard to his back door, and having nothing better to do because I hadn't gone to the pictures I followed him. You see, he left his back door open a bit, so I gave it a push and went in. I stood there, just watching him, sucking my thumb, the other hand in my pocket. I suppose he knew I was there, because his eyes were moving more natural now, but he didn't seem to mind. 'What are yer going to do wi' that rope, mate?' I asked him.

'I'm going ter 'ang messen, lad,' he told me, as though he'd done it a time or two already, and people had usually asked him questions like this beforehand.

'What for, mate?' He must have thought I was a nosy young bogger.

'Cause I want to, that's what for,' he said, clearing all the pots off the table and pulling it to the middle of the room. Then he stood on it to fasten the rope to the light-fitting. The table creaked and didn't look very safe, but it did him for what he wanted.

'It wain't hold up, mate,' I said to him, thinking how much better it was being here than sitting in the pictures and seeing the Jungle Jim serial.

But he got nettled now and turned on me. 'Mind yer own business.'

I thought he was going to tell me to scram, but he didn't. He made ever such a fancy knot with that rope, as though he'd been a sailor or summat, and as he tied it he was whistling a fancy tune to himself. Then he got down from the table and pushed it back to the wall, and put a chair in its place. He wasn't looking black at all, nowhere near as black as anybody in our family, when they're feeling fed-up. If ever he'd looked only half as black as our dad looked twice a week he'd have hanged himself years ago, I couldn't help thinking. But he was making a good job of that rope all right, as though he'd thought about it a lot anyway, and as though it was going to be the last thing he'd ever do. But I knew something he didn't know, because he wasn't standing where I was. I knew the rope wouldn't hold up, and I told him so, again.

'Shut yer gob,' he said, but quiet like, 'or I'll kick yer out.'

I didn't want to miss it, so I said nothing. He took his cap off and put it on the dresser, then he took his coat off, and his scarf, and spread them out on the sofa. I wasn't a bit frightened, like I might be now at sixteen, because it was interesting. And being only ten I'd never had a chance to see a bloke hang himself before. We got pally, the two of us, before he slipped the rope around his neck.

'Shut the door,' he asked me, and I did as I was told. 'Ye're a good lad for your age,' he said to me while I sucked my thumb, and he felt in his pockets and pulled out all that was inside, throwing the handful of bits and bobs on the table: fag-packet and peppermints, a pawn-ticket, an old comb, and a few coppers. He picked out a penny and gave it to me, saying: 'Now listen ter me, young 'un. I'm going to 'ang messen, and when I'm swinging I want you to gi' this chair a bloody good kick and push it away. All right?'

I nodded.

He put the rope around his neck, and then took it off like it was a tie that didn't fit. 'What are yer going to do it for, mate?' I asked again.

'Because I'm fed-up' he said, looking very unhappy. 'And because I want to. My missus left me, and I'm out o' work.'

I didn't want to argue, because the way he said it, I knew he couldn't do anything else except hang himself. Also there was a funny look in his face: even when he talked to me I swear he couldn't see me. It was different to the black looks my old man puts on, and I suppose that's why my old man would never hang himself, worse luck, because he never gets a look into his clock like this bloke had. My old man's look stares *at* you, so that you have to back down and fly out of the house: this bloke's look looked *through* you, so that you could face it and know it wouldn't do you any harm. So I saw now that dad would never hang himself because he could never get the right sort of look into his face, in spite of the fact that he'd been out of work often enough. Maybe mam would have to leave him first, and then he might do it; but no – I shook my head – there wasn't much chance of that even though he did lead her a dog's life.

'Yer wain't forget to kick that chair away?' he reminded me, and I swung my head to say I wouldn't. So my eyes were popping and I watched every move he made. He stood on the chair and put the rope around his neck so that it fitted this time, still whistling his fancy tune. I wanted to get a better goz at the knot, because my pal was in the Scouts, and would ask to know how it was done, and if I told him later he'd let me know what happened at the pictures in the Jungle Jim serial, so's I could have my cake and eat it as well, as mam says, tit for tat. But I thought I'd better not ask the bloke to tell me, and I stayed back in my corner. The last thing he did was take the wet dirty butt-end from his lips and sling it into the empty firegrate, following it with his eyes to the black fireback where it landed – as if he was then going to mend a fault in the lighting like any electrician.

Suddenly his long legs wriggled and his feet tried to kick the chair, so I helped him as I'd promised I would and took a runner at it as if I was playing centre-forward for Notts Forest, and the chair went scooting back against the sofa, dragging his muffler to the floor as it tipped over. He swung for a bit, his arms chafing like he was a scarecrow flapping birds away, and he made a noise in his throat as if he'd just took a dose of salts and was trying to make them stay down.

Then there was another sound, and I looked up and saw a big crack come in the ceiling, like you see on the pictures when an earthquake's happening, and the bulb began circling round and round as though it was a space ship. I was just beginning to get dizzy when, thank Christ, he fell down with such a horrible thump on the floor that I thought he'd broke every bone he'd got. He kicked around for a bit, like a dog that's got colic bad. Then he lay still.

I didn't stay to look at him. 'I told him that rope wouldn't hold up,' I kept saying to myself as I went out of the house, tut-tutting because he hadn't done the job right, hands stuffed deep into my pockets and nearly crying at the balls-up he'd made of everything. I slammed his gate so hard with disappointment that it nearly dropped off its hinges.

Just as I was going back up the yard to get my tea at home, hoping the others had come back from the pictures so's I wouldn't have anything to keep on being black about, a copper passed me and headed for the bloke's door. He was striding quickly with his head bent forward, and I knew that somebody had narked. They must have seen him buy the rope and then tipped-off the cop. Or happen the old hen at the yard-end had finally caught on. Or perhaps he'd even told somebody himself, because I supposed that the bloke who'd strung himself up hadn't much known what he was doing, especially with the look I'd seen in his eyes. But that's how it is, I said to myself, as I followed the copper back to the bloke's house, a poor bloke can't even hang himself these days.

When I got back the copper was slitting the rope from his neck with a pen-knife, then he gave him a drink of water, and the bloke opened his peepers. I didn't like the copper, because he'd got a couple of my mates sent to approved school for pinching lead piping from lavatories.

'What did you want to hang yourself for?' he asked the bloke, trying to make him sit up. He could hardly talk, and one his hands was bleeding from where the light-bulb had smashed. I knew that rope wouldn't hold up, but he hadn't listened to me. I'll never hang myself anyway, but if I want to I'll make sure I do it from a tree or something like that, not a light-fitting. 'Well, what did you do it for?'

'Because I wanted to,' the bloke croaked.

'You'll get five years for this,' the copper told him. I'd crept back into the house and was sucking my thumb in the same corner.

'That's what yo' think,' the bloke said, a normal frightened look in his eyes now. 'I only wanted to hang myself.'

'Well,' the copper said, taking out his book, 'It's against the law, you know.'

'Nay,' the bloke said, 'it can't be. It's my life, ain't it?'

'You might think so,' the copper said, 'but it ain't.'

He began to suck the blood from his hand. It was such a little scratch though that you couldn't see it. 'That's the first thing I knew,' he said.

'Well I'm telling you,' the copper told him.

'Course, I didn't let on to the copper that I'd helped the bloke to hang himself. I wasn't born yesterday, nor the day before yesterday either.

'It's a fine thing if a bloke can't tek his own life', the bloke said, seeing he was in for it.

'Well he can't,' the copper said, as if reading out of his book and enjoying it. 'It ain't your life. And it's a crime to take your own life. It's killing yourself. It's suicide.'

The bloke looked hard, as if every one of the copper's words meant six-months cold. I felt sorry for him, and that's a fact, but if only he'd listened to what I'd said and not depended on that light-fitting. He should have done it from a tree, or something like that.

He went up the yard with the copper like a peaceful lamb, and we all thought that that was the end of that.

But a couple of days later the news was flashed through to us – even before it got to the *Post* because a woman in our yard worked at the hospital of an evening dishing grub out and tidying up. I heard her spilling it to somebody at the yard-end. 'I'd never 'ave thought it. I thought he'd got that daft idea out of his head when they took him away. But no. Wonders'll never cease. Chucked 'issen from the hospital window when the copper who sat near his bed went off for a pee. Would you believe it? Dead? Not much 'e ain't.'

He'd heaved himself at the glass, and fallen like a stone on to the road. In one way I was sorry he'd done it, but in another I was glad, because he'd proved to the coppers and everybody whether it was his life or not all right. It was marvellous though, the way the brainless bastards had put him in a ward six floors up, which finished him off, proper, even better than a tree.

All of which will make me think twice about how black I sometimes feel. The black coal-bag locked inside you, and the black look it puts on your face, doesn't mean you're going to string yourself up or sling yourself under a double-decker or chuck yourself out of a window or cut your throat with a sardine-tin or put your head in the gas-oven or drop your rotten sack-bag of a body on to a railway line, because when you're feeling that black you can't even move from your chair. Anyhow, I know I'll never get so black as to hang myself, because hanging don't look very nice to me, and never will, the more I remember old what's-his-name swinging from the light-fitting.

More than anything else, I'm glad now I didn't go to the pictures that Saturday afternoon when I was feeling black and ready to do myself in. Because you know, I shan't ever kill myself. Trust me, I'll stay alive half-barmy till I'm a hundred and five, and then go out screaming blue murder because I want to stay where I am.

Alan Sillitoe

21

Suicides

Reading the evening papers we meet them,
Those anonymous names:
She who turned the gas on her sorrow,
He whom the Thames
Left one night more derelict on its shore
Than a child at the convent door.

Little we knew them, these who in their lives
Rated no column.
And even now only between the lines
May we glimpse the solemn
Dilemmas that drove them thither and guess
Something of their last loneliness.

What of this girl? Surely her beauty might
Have confounded the shades?
Or was it beauty itself that led her
Into the glades
Of darkness, where, by love's fever oppressed,
She sought to be dispossessed?

And what of him they found in the chilly dawn
With the tide in his hair?
They say in drowning a man unravels all
His history there
In a fleeting moment, before he falls away
On eternal silence. So he may

Have found at last in some long-sought, half-forgotten
Memory a mirror
Reflecting his first true self, distorted since
By childhood terror.
Oh then perhaps – the pattern revealed – too late
He saw his meaningless fate....

We cannot know. For even the notes they left
In their desolate rooms
Can tell us little but that our restless souls
To unknown dooms
Move on; while still, deep in each human face,
We seek the signature of grace.

Tragic their deaths, more tragic the aching thought
That had we been there
We might have laid our hands on their hands and begged
'Do not despair!
For here, even here in this living touch, this breath,
May be the solace you seek in death.'

J. C. Hall

22

Not Waving But Drowning

Nobody heard him, the dead man,
But still he lay moaning:
He was much farther out than you thought
And not waving but drowning.

Poor chap, he always loved larking
And now he's dead
It must have been too cold for him his heart gave way,
They said.

Oh no, no, no, it was too cold always
(Still the dead one lay moaning)
I was much too far out all my life
And not waving but drowning.

Stevie Smith

23

Ledge Psychology

We have had a problem lately in Chicago with people jumping off ledges. We've always had a problem with people jumping off ledges in Chicago and so many so that the Police Department has come up with a regulation on how to handle a guy on a ledge, see. You know, the patrolman on the beat. The first point is – never go out on the ledge in your uniform, you see, because the image of authority may be *just* the reason they're out there to begin with. Secondly, you should be very casual and never issue direct commands to 'em, you see, never antagonise them. And third, and this is really, I suppose, a main point, be completely unsympathetic, because basically they wanna be talked out of it. So I would like to present a Chicago policeman under this new regulation – he sees a guy on a ledge, he slips into a sports jacket, and I think he would probably light a cigarette then he would walk out on the ledge something like this...

Oh hi....You, er, you thinking about jumping, are you? Your first time is it?

* * * *

Me? No, no, I'm on my way to work, as a matter of fact. I usually walk round the ledges, I find it kinda . . . helps me unwind. You, er, you don't happen to be in advertising, by any chance, do you?

* * * *

Yeah, it was more of a lucky guess. We get a lot of advertising people out here....Oh, which way did you come out, by the way, did you come out through the window or did you come around the corner the building? The reason I ask — there are two other advertising guys on the south-east corner, I thought maybe...

* * * *

No, as a matter of fact I didn't get their names, er, I think one

guy had the Etzell account or sumpin like that . . . you know,
you're drawing a helluva crowd for a weekday.

* * * *

Yeah, really. The last couple of years jumping has, has really fallen off . . . ha, ha, ha . . . I didn't mean it that way, I . . . no, really, seriously, you take 1929, for example, you literally couldn't get out on this ledge in 1929. . . . No we had people lined up in the corridors just waiting to get out on the ledge. Finally, we finally went to that numbered card system they use in the butcher's shops. . . . Well, you see that, the cart down there – the hot-dog stand? That's Sam, the hot-dog man. Hi, Sam, how are you . . . how's the wife? I was just tellin' him – helluva crowd for a Thursday, isn't it? Listen, have you eaten, by the way?

* * * *

Don't be silly. Er, two, Sam

* * * *

You want everything on it?

* * * *

Two. Two with everything, Sam.

* * * *

No, no. To go, Sam, to go. Oho, oho, some fink turned you in.

* * * *

Yeah, you see, you see the guys with the net down there....

* * * *

Yep ... they're firemen.

* * * *

Yeah. Eh ... Oh, I'll give you a little tip there. Move away to the corner of the building, you see, then they'll start to follow you, then you run back here and jump.

* * * *

Well, they get all confused and they start pulling all different directions – and they'll never make it back in time, believe me.

* * * *

Don't be silly – I'm glad to do it for you. Now listen, gee, I really ought to be getting to work, you know. . . I'd love to stay around and catch it ...

* * * *

No, don't be silly ... er ... take your own sweet time about it.

* * * *

Yeah, that is a long way down, isn't it? ... You, em, you kinda chickening out now, um? That happens quite a bit. . . you, er, you have a certain responsibility to those people down there, though, I . . . Some of them bin there a half hour or so you know.

* * * *

No, no, it's up to you, I mean, er ... if you don't want to, you know, you don't have to.

* * * *

Well, all right. It's your. . . . Well, listen I'll get in, an', and then you follow me, all right?

* * * *

Okay. Oh, er, one ... Now where the hell did he go?

Bob Newhart

24

Of Mice and Men

...Then two men emerged from the path and came into the opening by the green pool. They had walked in single file down the path, and even in the open one stayed behind the other. Both were dressed in denim trousers and in denim coats with brass buttons. Both wore black shapeless hats and both carried tight blanket rolls slung over their shoulders. The first man was small and quick, dark of face, with restless eyes and sharp, strong features. Every part of him was defined: small, strong hands, slender arms, a thin and bony nose. Behind him walked his opposite, a huge man, shapeless of face, with large, pale eyes, with wide, sloping shoulders; and he walked heavily, dragging his feet a little, the way a bear drags his paws. His arms did not swing at his sides, but hung loosely and only moved because the heavy hands were pendula.

*   *   *

George said, 'I want you to stay with me, Lennie. Jesus Christ, somebody'd shoot you for a coyote[1] if you was by yourself. No, you stay with me. Your Aunt Clara wouldn't like you running off by yourself, even if she is dead.'

Lennie spoke craftily: 'Tell me like you done before.'
'Tell you what?'

[1] coyote: a prairie wolf, found in North America

'About the rabbits.'

George snapped, 'You ain't gonna put nothing over on me.'

Lennie pleaded, 'Come on, George. Tell me. Please, George. Like you done before.'

'You get a kick outta that, don't you? A'right. I'll tell you, and then we'll eat our supper. . . .'

George's voice became deeper. He repeated his words rhythmically as though he had said them many times before. 'Guys like us, that work on ranches, are the loneliest guys in the world. They got no family. They don't belong no place. They come to a ranch an' work up a stake and then they go inta town and blow their stake, and the first thing you know they're poundin' their tail on some other ranch. They ain't got nothing to look ahead to.'

Lennie was delighted. 'That's it, that's it. Now tell how it is with us.'

George went on. 'With us it ain't like that. We got a future. We got somebody to talk to that gives a damn about us. We don't have to sit in no bar-room blowin' in our jack jus' because we got no place else to go. If them other guys gets in jail they can rot for all anybody gives a damn. But not us.'

Lennie broke in. *'But not us! An' why? Because ... because I got you to look after me, and you got me to look after you, and that's why.'* He laughed delightedly. 'Go on now, George.'

'You got it by heart. You can do it yourself.'

'No; you. I forget some a' the things. Tell about how it's gonna be.'

'O.K. Some day we're gonna get the jack together and we're gonna have a little house and a couple of acres an' a cow and some pigs and ...'

'An' live off the fatta the lan',' Lennie shouted. 'An' have *rabbits*. Go on, George! Tell about what we're gonna have in the garden and about the rabbits in the cages and about the rain in the winter and the stove, and how thick the cream is on the milk like you can hardly cut it. Tell about that, George.'

'Why'n't you do it yourself. You know all of it.'

'No . . . you tell it. It ain't the same if I tell it. Go on. . . . George. How I get to tend the rabbits.

'Well,' said George. 'We'll have a big vegetable patch and a rabbit-hutch and chickens. And when it rains in the winter, we'll just say the hell with goin' to work, and we'll build up a fire in the stove and set around it an' listen to the rain comin' down on the roof. Nuts!' He took out his pocket-knife. 'I ain't got time for no more.' He drove his knife through the top of one of the bean-cans, sawed out the top and passed the can to Lennie. Then he opened a second can. From his side pocket he brought out two spoons and passed one of them to Lennie.

They sat by the fire and filled their mouths with beans and chewed mightily. A few beans slipped out of the side of Lennie's mouth. George gestured with his spoon. 'What you gonna say tomorrow when the boss asks you questions?'

Lennie stopped chewing and swallowed. His face was concentrated. 'I ... I ain't gonna ... say a word.'

'Good boy! That's fine, Lennie! Maybe you're gettin' better. When we get the coupla acres I can let you tend the rabbits all right. 'Specially if you remember as good as that.'

Lennie choked with pride. 'I can remember, ' he said.

George motioned with his spoon again.

'Look, Lennie. I want you to look around here. You can remember this place, can't you? The ranch is about a quarter-mile up that way. Just follow the river.'

'Sure,' said Lennie. 'I can remember this. Di'n't I remember about not gonna says a word?'

'Course you did. Well, Lennie, if you jus' happen to get in trouble like you always done before, I want you to come right here an' hide in the brush.'

'Hide in the brush,' said Lennie slowly.

'Hide in the brush till I come for you. Can you remember that?'

'Sure I can, George. Hide in the brush till you come.'

'But you ain't gonna get in no trouble, because if you do, I won't let you tend the rabbits.' He threw his empty bean can off into the brush.

'I won't get in no trouble, George. I ain't gonna say a word.'

'O.K. Bring your bindle over here by the fire. It's gonna be nice sleepin' here. Lookin' up, and the leaves. Don't build up no more fire. We'll let her die down.'

They made their beds on the sand, and as the blaze dropped from the fire the sphere of light grew smaller; the curling branches disappeared and only a faint glimmer showed where the treetrunks were.

John Steinbeck

The Rebel

When everybody has short hair,
The rebel lets his hair grow long.

When everybody has long hair,
The rebel cuts his hair short.

When everybody talks during the lesson,
The rebel doesn't say a word.

When nobody talks during the lesson,
The rebel creates a disturbance.

When everybody wears a uniform,
The rebel dresses in fantastic clothes.

When everybody wears fantastic clothes,
The rebel dresses soberly.

In the company of dog lovers,
The rebel expresses a preference for cats.

In the company of cat lovers,
The rebel puts in a good word for dogs.

When everybody is praising the sun,
The rebel remarks on the need for rain.

When everybody is greeting the rain,
The rebel regrets the absence of sun.

When everybody goes to the meeting,
The rebel stays at home and reads a book.

When everybody stays at home and reads a book,
The rebel goes to the meeting.

When everybody says, Yes please,
The rebel says, No thank you.

When everybody says, No thank you,
The rebel says, Yes please.

It is very good that we have rebels,
You may not find it very good to be one.

D.J. Enright

26

Let Me Die
a Youngman's Death

Let me die a youngman's death
not a clean & in between
the sheets holywater death
not a clean & inbetween
peaceful out of breath death

When I'm 73
& in constant good tumour
may I be mown down at dawn
by a bright red sports car
on my way home
from an allnight party

Or when I'm 91
with silver hair
& sitting in a barber's chair
may rival gangsters
with hamfisted tommyguns burst in
& give me a short back and insides

Or when I'm 104
& banned from the Cavern
may my mistress
catching me in bed with her daughter
& fearing her son
cut me up into little pieces
& throw away every piece but one

Let me die a youngman's death
not a free from sin tiptoe in
candle wax & waning death
not a curtains drawn by angels borne
'what a nice way to go' death

Roger McGough

27

The Lapse

At 4.13 Henry showed his season ticket to the porter and climbed into the railway car. He nodded politely to Miss Burge, the teacher at the kindergarten, who sat in her corner seat knitting the green jumper she had started last month; and to the district nurse in her black pork-pie hat, her professional bag tucked warmly against her stomach. They both smiled back – nothing said, never anything said – and he went to his usual place at the far end of the car. He filled his pipe while waiting for the train to start, and then put it back into his pocket.

Back and fore, back and fore, like a shuttle, workwards each morning, homewards each night, ra-ta-ta, ra-ta-ta, the train's travelling beat – how many times have I done this journey, these last five years? If I put the journeys end to end it would stretch a long way – right into Tibet perhaps, along the Turk-Sib, among the moujiks[1]... Oh dear! Henry yawned and gazed indifferently at the row of slatternly back gardens and flapping clothes lines past which the train ran. Twice a day for five years, Bank holidays excepted, those drab hotch-potch backs where the wives riddled yesterday's ashes and the children sat on the steps eating bread and jam. It was so depressing to see those streets every day, always the same, and the people always the same – how many of them knew they had been condemned to serve a lifer?

And then, with a rattle and a wrench, the open country; the hills swooping like swallows. Below the embankment the black river swirled, wandering down from the coal mines at the head of the valley. And the train rattled over the bridge that spanned the river; Henry felt the drop under the bridge, sheer and empty in the pit of his stomach, like a bird flashing through a hollow cave. And on, accelerando, through the cutting. What shall I do to-night, the tired voice asked in his head. Pictures? Or a nap and a stroll down to the billiard hall? I don't know what to do, I can never make up my mind. I know what'll happen – I'll stand by my bedroom window

---

[1] moujiks: Russian peasants

looking down into the empty street. And in the end I won't go out. I'll waste the night, as usual, as I waste everything. I ought to decide to *do* something, to get *on* ... One day I *will* do something, to justify all this waste, something grand, careless ... I *must* ...

I wonder what's for dinner this evening? Mother will have it all ready, whatever it is, warmed up and waiting; and she'll sit opposite me while I eat it, watching me wolf it; and at the end she'll have a cup of tea with me ... Doctor said she's alright. But often I dream she is dead, and I wake up sweating.

Halt number one. The schoolgirl comes in and sits where she always sits, and takes a book out of her satchel, a different book this week. She has grown a lot in the last five years. She used to be a scrimpy, flat-chested little thing, her head always poked out of the window; now she sits absorbed in her book and there is a difference about everything she does. She must be about sixteen; she hardly looks it, with her mouse-bitten fringe and her black stockings. She's got a strange face; those who don't know her would never call it pretty. They'd only see her prominent top teeth, her weak chin, her flat cheekbones. They'd miss the secret quality, the look she has when she turns from her book to look out through the window. She's pulling on her woollen gloves; she gets out at the next halt. I wish I knew where she lives – in the semi-detached red-roofed houses on the right, or the huddle of slums on the left? Not that it matters really; the train always starts off before she's left the platform. Sometimes, if she hasn't finished her chapter before the train stops, she walks along the platform with her book open …

The little woman who only travels on Thursdays is snoring; she always puts her feet up and snoozes. Her head hangs forward, her oak-apple nose nearly dropping into her shopping basket, her pink umbrella laid across her lap. Her shoes need soling. Oh, curse it and curse it. It's always, always the same, daunting you properly. Makes you want to smash the window, pull the communication cord, scream … And instead you swallow the scream; you can hear it struggling inside you, battering at the door of your throat. And you sit still, and look at the old lady's brown hat, and Miss Burge knitting, and *her* reading. It's been lovely, really, watching her grow up, wondering about her, her name and what she thinks when she's reading and what Life will do to her, and feeling sorry for her, somehow …

The train stopped with a shudder that rattled all the windows. The red roofs and the biscuit facades of the new houses waited faithfully outside. The girl closed her book and obediently went out.

And then, all of a sudden, Henry got up and walked down the car, past Miss Burge and the district nurse, who stared at him in astonishment. The blood was beating like a steel hammer behind his eyes. He fumbled and tugged at the carriage door. But he got out, and was standing on the ash platform, for the first time, ever. She was a few yards ahead of him, finishing her chapter, walking slowly, unaware. He

stepped forward. The porter shouted 'O.K.' to the guard. The engine-driver leaned over the footplate. Henry stood stock still, looking at the girl, at the railings, at the yellow advertisement of Duck, Son and Pinker's pianos. The guard shouted 'What are you getting off here for?' The green flag and the engine's hoot . . . Henry scrambled back into the carriage, the guard shouted at him and a porter blasphemed. He shut the door with quivering hands and slouched back to his seat. Miss Burge and the nurse stared at him and at each other. He didn't notice anything. He just slumped into his seat and clenched his hands, squeezing them between his knees. After a couple of minutes he blew his nose hard and rubbed some smuts out of his eyes. The train crashed into the black mouth of the tunnel with a shriek. It woke the old lady. She opened her eyes and tidied her collar, as if it were the most natural thing in the world to open one's eyes, after they have been closed.

The train came out of the tunnel and stopped. The old lady picked up her basket and her pink umbrella, Miss Burge rolled up her knitting, the nurse fingered the silver hairpin that skewered her pork-pie hat. Henry followed them out onto the platform and slunk past the guard like a criminal.

Alun Lewis

82

Elephant

It is quite unfair to be
obliged to be large, so I suppose
you could call me discontented.

Think big, they said, when
I was a little elephant; they
wanted me to get used to it.

It was kind. But it doesn't help if,
inside, you are carefree in small ways,
fond of little amusements.

You are smaller than me, think
how conveniently near the flowers are,
how you can pat the cat by just

halfbending over. You can also
arrange teacups for dolls, play
marbles in the proper season.

I would give anything to be
able to do a tiny, airy, flitting
dance to show how very little a

thing happiness can be really.

Alan Brownjohn

The Plaint of the Camel

Canary-birds feed on sugar and seed
   Parrots have crackers to crunch;
And as for the poodles, they tell me the noodles
   Have chicken and cream for their lunch.
      But there's never a question
      About MY digestion –
  ANYTHING does for me!

Cats, you're aware, can repose in a chair,
   Chickens can roost upon rails,
Puppies are able to sleep in a stable
   And oysters can slumber in pails
      But none supposes
      A poor camel doses –
  ANY PLACE does for me!

Lambs are enclosed where it's never exposed,
   Coops are constructed for hens;
Kittens are treated to houses well-heated,
   And pigs are protected by pens.
      But a camel comes handy
      Wherever it's sandy –
  ANYWHERE does for me!

People would laugh if you rode a giraffe,
    Or mounted the back of an ox;
It's nobody's habit to ride on a rabbit,
    Or try to bestraddle a fox.
        But as for a camel, he's
        Ridden by families –
    ANY LOAD does for me!

A snake is as round as a hole in the ground;
    Weasels are wavy and sleek;
And no alligator could ever be straighter
    Than lizards that live in a creek.
        But a camel's all lumpy
        And bumpy and humpy –
    ANY SHAPE does for me!

                    Charles Edward Carryl

30

New Readers Begin Here

You would never think it to meet her, but Bella cannot read. She is a cheerful, talkative young grandmother, happily married, and has worked all her life in factories, shops and as a restaurant cook, but until about a year ago written words did not exist for her. As a child she had bad eyesight and her mother was advised not to let her use her eyes too much. So at school she sat where she could not see the blackboard and, whenever there was a chore to be done, young Bella was sent. Once a child starts slipping behind in reading, and if no one makes a special effort to retrieve the straggler, then it is probable that the deficiency will be a lifelong handicap for him or her. 'They think you're just an idiot,' she said. 'But you're not.'

She showed clearly that she was not in the years after school, managing to live a generally happy life in a world of printed directions, signs, forms, letters and newspapers, none of which meant anything. 'You had to bluff your way through.'

If she went for a job and they handed her a form she would say, 'Oh, I've left my other glasses at home.' Working in shops, she would memorise where everything was and invent an excuse if some item had been moved. On train journeys she asked how many stops ahead her destination was and counted them off. Even when her husband was courting her, she did not dare tell him the truth and used to sit pretending to take in the newspaper. There were times, she told me, 'when I used to sit in shame.' Only after she was Mrs Bella Pocock did she confess. But, though her husband would always help her, she often found she was still too ashamed to ask. When he was in the army, her greatest deprivation was 'knowing I couldn't sit down and write a letter,' and that he had to confine himself to things a friendly neighbour could read. When they had children it was even worse if they brought a note home from school or asked her to read to them.

Even with friends who knew of her disability it was bad. She remembers with pain how, when postcards would arrive at places where she worked, no one would stop to read them to her. 'People think you're just not interested.' And, deprived of knowing what was in the papers, she felt herself cut off from others' ordinary concerns. 'You've got no conversation.'

Television, when it came, was a help. Though Bella says that, if it is your only source of interesting information, it is surprising how little use it is. Yet television eventually brought her the first glimpse of hope.

31

Slow Reader

He can make sculptures
And fabulous machines
Invent games, tell jokes
Give solemn, adult advice
But he is slow to read.
When I take him on my knee
With his *Ladybird* book
He gazes into the air
Sighing and shaking his head
Like an old man
Who knows the mountains
Are impassable.

He toys with words
Letting them grow cold
As gristly meat
Until I relent
And let him wriggle free –
A fish returning
To its element
Or a white-eyed colt
Shying from the bit
As if he sees
That if he takes it
In his mouth
He'll never run
Quite free again.

Vicki Feaver

32

Gipsy Peg

They are fewer than they were. But you can still see them – bright caravans parked on the edges of lonely country lanes. Horses hobbled nearby. Dark, barefoot children playing games with bright-eyed dogs. The gipsies. What is it like to be a gipsy? Why do they lead their wandering life? What do they talk about, and how do they live in this modern changing world?

Peg is everyone's idea of what a gipsy looks like – long, dark hair, shrewd, brown eyes, a gay pinafore over an Edwardian-length skirt, and jangling ear-rings.

She told me she had not slept in a house since she was sixteen, when she married. She has 15 children, 28 grand-children, and 2 great-grandchildren.

She has travelled all over England, but always comes back regularly to Buckinghamshire. 'We're Bucks people,' she explained. 'Gipsies like to have a county of their own.'

Life in the past was hard, but good. Her husband – he died four years ago – made flowers from wood shavings, which they hawked from door to door. They picked fruit and hops for farmers, 'chopped' (bought and sold) horses.

'You saw life then,' she said. 'When you finished in one place you packed up and went somewhere else. But now with all this building there's no place for gipsies.

'Most farmers don't want us because they're getting machinery. The local councils say we're a nuisance and won't let us camp. They fine us if we stop anywhere.

'I'm all right here because the boys can work on a farm. I can stop as long as I like. I'm one of the lucky people.

'At my time of life I'd be happy with one of those perma-nent sites they're supposed to be building for us – with a bit of garden and plenty of water. But I don't want no house. I want to feel I can just pack up and go when the fancy takes me – that's gipsy outlook. It's what you gorgios [non-gipsies] can't understand.'

She took me into her spotlessly neat caravan. 'See, it's small, but it don't feel small or stifling. Whenever I go into a house I want to choke. I keep wanting to yell: "Why don't you open all these windows?"

'People say we're dirty,' Peg said indignantly. 'Don't you believe it, sir. Most of us is cleaner than the likes of you – no offence meant.

'We've all got our own cups. No one – not even my husband – has ever drunk from mine. And the one you had is kept only for visitors.

'As to washing, all my family wash themselves from head to foot every day.

'We're religious too, I wouldn't wash in soapsuds on Good Friday. They say a gipsy woman did that once – and the washing water turned to blood. And I never wash blankets in May – gipsies think it would wash the family away.

'But times has changed,' Peg went on. 'I can remember when I daren't sit in front of a strange man and show even a bit of ankle. My husband would have been mad. And he hasn't been dead that long, you know.'

'Is it true,' I asked, 'that gipsies don't mind if their children can't read or write?'

'Some of mine went to school for a time,' Peg said, 'but they didn't learn much. They can't read or write – and that's a bit troublesome when you've papers to sign.

'But ask them how many rows of peas there are in a field, how many farthings in a hundred pound, and they'll tell you – just like that.'

She pointed through the doorway at a pair of gumbooted legs under an old car. 'That's one of mine – can't read a word, but he can take that car to bits and build it up again – can't you son?' A tousled-haired young man wriggled from under the car and grinned at her.

Gipsy Peg tells fortunes at the Derby and Ascot. 'That's the one thing about gipsy life that won't change,' she said. 'We'll be dunkerin' along after we've settled down on fixed sites.'

'Are you in a fortune-telling mood today?' I asked.

The effect of the question was amazing. The children and even the dogs took to their heels. In two seconds I was alone with Gipsy Peg and her crystal.

'It's not for the papers, mind,' she warned.

I assured her I would reveal nothing.

We talked for about fifteen minutes. I cannot tell whether old Peg had real divining powers, but if what she told me about myself was mere guesswork, all I can say is that she had an uncanny knack of guessing right.

The sun was setting as Gipsy Peg walked with me to the

edge of the lane to say good-bye. Behind the curtained windows of her caravan oil lamps flickered.

Peg pointed to a vast new council estate springing up a few fields away. 'That's what is spoiling it all,' she told me. 'There's nowhere for us to camp these days. It's all the building and those gorgio caravan-dwellers who give us a bad name.'

For a moment she listened to the hum of traffic from a distant main road, her eyes wistful. Then she turned and walked slowly back to her caravan.

Lewis de Fries

Gipsy

I, the man with the red scarf,
   Will give thee what I have, this last week's earnings.
Take them and buy thee a silver ring
   And wed me, to ease my yearnings.

For the rest, when thou art wedded
   I'll wet my brow for thee
With sweat, I'll enter a house for thy sake,
   Thou shalt shut doors on me.

D. H. Lawrence

34

The Test

On the afternoon Marian took her second driver's test, Mrs Ericson went with her. 'It's probably better to have someone a little older with you,' Mrs Ericson said as Marian slipped into the driver's seat beside her. 'Perhaps the last time your Cousin Bill made you nervous, talking too much on the way.'

'Yes, Ma'am,' Marian said in her soft unaccented voice. 'They probably do like it better if a white person shows up with you.'

'Oh, I don't think it's *that*,' Mrs Ericson began, and subsided after a glance at the girl's set profile. Marian drove the car slowly through the shady suburban streets. It was on the first hot days of June, and when they reached the boulevard they found it crowded with cars headed for the beaches.

'Do you want me to drive?' Mrs Ericson asked. 'I'll be glad to if you're feeling jumpy.' Marian shook her head. Mrs Ericson watched her dark, competent hands and wondered for the thousandth time how the house had ever managed to get along without her, or how she had lived through those earlier years when her household had been presided over by a series of slatternly white girls who had considered housework demeaning and the care of children an added insult. 'You drive beautifully, Marian,' she said. 'Now don't think of the last time. Anybody would slide on a steep hill on a wet day like that.'

'It takes four mistakes to flunk you,' Marian said. 'I don't remember doing all the things the inspector marked down on my blank.'

'People say that they only want you to slip them a little something,' Mrs Ericson said doubtfully.

'No,' Marian said. 'That would only make it worse, Mrs Ericson, I know.'

The car turned right, at a traffic signal, into a side road and slid up to the curb at the rear of a short line of parked cars. The inspectors had not arrived yet.

'You have the papers?' Mrs Ericson asked. Marian took them out of her bag: her learner's permit, the car registration, and her birth certificate. They settled down to the dreary business of waiting.

'It will be marvellous to have someone dependable to drive the children to school every day,' Mrs Ericson said.

Marian looked up from the list of driving requirements she had been studying. 'It'll make things simpler at the house, won't it?' she said.

'Oh, Marian,' Mrs Ericson exclaimed, 'if I could only pay you half of what you're worth!'

'Now, Mrs Ericson,' Marian said firmly. They looked at each other and smiled with affection.

Two cars with official insignia on their doors stopped across the street. The inspectors leaped out, very brisk and military in their neat uniforms. Marian's hands tightened on the wheel. 'There's the one who flunked me last time,' she whispered, pointing to a stocky, self-important man who had begun to shout directions at the driver at the head of the line. 'Oh, Mrs Ericson.'

'Now, Marian,' Mrs Ericson said. They smiled at each other again, rather weakly.

The inspector who finally reached their car was not the stocky one but a genial, middle-aged man who grinned broadly as he thumbed over their papers. Mrs Ericson started to get out of the car. 'Don't you want to come along?' the inspector asked. 'Mandy and I don't mind company.'

Mrs Ericson was bewildered for a moment. 'No,' she said, and stepped to the curb. 'I might make Marian self-conscious. She's a fine driver, Inspector.'

'Sure thing,' the inspector said, winking at Mrs Ericson. He slid into the seat beside Marian.

'Turn right at the corner, Mandy-Lou.'

From the curb, Mrs Ericson watched the car move smoothly up the street.

The inspector made notations in a small black book. 'Age?' he enquired presently as they drove along.

'Twenty-seven.'

He looked at Marian out of the corner of his eye. 'Old enough to have a quite a flock of pickaninnies, eh?'

Marian did not answer.

'Left at this corner,' the inspector said, 'and park between that truck and the green Buick.'

The two cars were very close together, but Marian squeezed in between them without too much manoeuvring.

'Driven before, Mandy-Lou?' the inspector asked.

'Yes, sir, I had a licence for three years in Pennsylvania.'

'Why do you want to drive a car?'

'My employer needs me to take her children to and from school.'

'Sure you don't really want to sneak out nights to meet some young blood?' the inspector asked. He laughed as Marian shook her head.

'Let's see you take a left at the corner and then turn around in the middle of the next block,' the inspector said. He began to whistle 'Swanee River'. 'Make you homesick?' he asked.

Marian put out her hand, swung around neatly in the street, and headed back in the direction from which they had come. 'No,' she said, 'I was born in Scranton, Pennsylvania.'

The inspector feigned astonishment. 'You-all ain't Southern?' he said. 'Well, dog my cats if I didn't think you-all came from down yondah.'

'No sir,' Marian said.

Turn onto Main Street and let's see how you-all does in heavier traffic.'

They followed a line of cars along Main Street for several blocks until they came in sight of a concrete bridge which arched high over the railway tracks.

'Read that sign at the end of the bridge,' the inspector said.

'Proceed with caution. Dangerous in slippery weather,' Marian said.

'You-all sho can read fine,' the inspector exclaimed. 'Where d'you learn to read like that, Mandy?'

'I got my college degree last year,' Marian said. Her voice was not quite steady.

As the car crept up the slope of the bridge the inspector burst out laughing. He laughed so hard he could scarcely give his next direction. 'Stop here,' he said, wiping his eyes, 'then start 'er up again. Mandy got her degree, did she? Dog my cats!'

Marian pulled up beside the curb. She put the car in neutral, pulled on the emergency, waited a moment, and then put the car into gear again. Her face was set. As she released the brake her foot slipped off the clutch pedal and the engine stalled.

'Now, Mistress Mandy,' the inspector said, 'remember your degree.'

'*Damn* you!' Marian cried. She started the car with a jerk.

The inspector lost his joviality in an instant.

'Return to the starting place, please,' he said, and made four very black crosses at random in the squares on Marian's application blank.

Mrs Ericson was waiting at the curb where they had left her. As Marian stopped the car, the inspector jumped out and brushed past her, his face purple.

'What's happened?' Mrs Ericson asked, looking after him with alarm.

Marian stared down at the wheel and her lip trembled.

'Oh, Marian, *again*?' Mrs Ericson said.

Marian nodded. 'In a sort of different way,' she said, and slid over to the right-hand side of the car.

Angelica Gibbs

35

We have never been free

I was born in South Africa. My early fore-fathers were born here. They were here long before there were any white-skinned people here. God put them here.

Still, I cannot worship where I want to.
I cannot learn where I want to.
I cannot marry whom I want to.
I cannot go where I want to or live where I want to.
I cannot even be buried where I want to when I die.

I cannot do these things because in the mind of the white-skinned people of South Africa I am not a human being. I am not South African. I am 'Coloured'.

What is a 'Coloured'? We are an accident in history – the result of the passionate meeting of white-skinned rovers from Europe and the yellow-skinned Hottentot women they found at the southernmost tip of Africa. That was our beginning, and we were born into slavery. We are the only people who have never really been free. We are close to the whites because our 'culture' is white, but they discriminate against us because our skins are dark. We are told by the blacks that we belong with them because our skins are dark, but they distrust us because our 'culture' is white. Both need us.

I was visited last night by an agent for a life insurance company who is determined to sign me up. But he won't because he has told me that my premium will be higher than the premium of a white man who takes the same policy. Because I am 'Coloured'. Apparently 'statistics' show the insurance companies that whites live longer than 'Coloureds' and therefore they pay less.

I am stripped, in a sense, of my manhood. I sit in a bus in which some seats are 'reserved' for 'us' and most for 'them'. A woman, one of 'them' boards the bus. All 'their' seats are filled. And so are 'ours'. She is an old woman and none of 'them' gives her a seat. I want to but I cannot because she belongs to 'them'. So I sit and she stands. It is the law. *They* made it for me. But *they* suffer from it too, sometimes.

School: My son is impatient to go to school. But I cannot send him to school until he is seven years old. White children can go when they are six years old. Even earlier. But 'statistics' have proved that my son is mentally ready only when he is seven years old.

I am standing in the Caledon Square police station (Cape Town), waiting to pay a traffic fine. They bring in a white man. He is a hobo. He is drunk and covered with blood. He smells like a rotten fish and the spittle runs down his matted beard. He asks for a glass of water. The white sergeant turns to a 'Coloured' sergeant and commands, 'Bring the baas a glass of water'.

I walk out of the police station. My anger, resentment, chokes me. Is it hatred? I do not know, but it is getting worse. I know it is getting dangerous. For all of us. Them and us. I would like to say, 'Please stop. This cannot go on'. But they will not allow me to warn them. If I do, I will be called an agitator, a Communist. So I do not say what is on my mind. But I scheme. And all my schemes are against them.

They have made me 'Coloured'. *They* make me live like a 'Coloured'. But there is a difference between my 'Coloured' and *their* 'Coloured'. I feel oppressed. I no longer feel that I am a part of *them*. They have forfeited their right to hold my hand in the journey into the future, for they have made it clear to me that they suppress every human desire and emotion in me because I am 'Coloured' in their eyes.

We have time on our side, time to find out that we do not need to rely on the white man for everything. We can do much ourselves. Each of us must become our brother's keeper until the white man feels that he is alone and that he cannot continue without us. He must learn to know that our heartbeats make this country of ours endure. He must learn that every law he makes which is designed to rob us of our destiny as human beings holds him back too and prevents him from growing from 'white man' to 'man'. And when the cost of it all gets home to the lowliest one of them, we will have won our struggle and I and my brown-skinned brothers will no longer be 'Coloured' men but men together with them and the blacks.

Howard Lawrence, Newsweek, 10 May, 1971

36

Streets of London

Have you seen the old man in the closed-down market,
Kicking up the papers with his worn out shoes?
In his eyes you see no pride, hands held loosely by his side,
Yesterday's paper telling yesterday's news.

Chorus
So how can you tell me you're lonely,
And say for you that the sun don't shine?
Let me take you by the hand and lead you through the streets
* of London*
I'll show you something to make you change your mind.

Have you seen the old girl who walks the streets of London?
Dirt in her hair and her clothes in rags?
She's no time for talkin' she just keeps right on walkin'
Carrying her home in two carrier bags.

In the all-night café at a quarter past eleven,
Same old man sitting there on his own,
Looking at the world over the rim of his teacup,
Each tea lasts an hour and he wanders home alone.

Have you seen the old man outside the seaman's mission,
Memory fading with the medal ribbons that he wears?
In our winter city the rain cries a little pity
For one more forgotten hero and a world that doesn't care.

Ralph McTell

37

Snowscene

snow crackles under foot
like powdered bones
trees have dandruff
in their hair
and the wind moans
    the wind moans

ponds are wearing glasses
with lenses three feet deep
birds are silent in the air
as stones
and the wind can't sleep
    the wind can't sleep

i found an old man by the road
who had not long been dead
i had not heard his lonely groans
nor seen him weep
only birds heard the last words he said
before the wind pulled a sheet o'er his head
    the wind pulled a sheet o'er his head

Roger McGough

38

The Car

EARL *is standing at the top of the quarry. He gives an expansive cough.*

EARL: Ah, 'tis a fine day to contemplate the world from such a lofty view.

> LUKE *comes to, and makes as though to run off.*

EARL: Don't run off, young man. I'm not the Devil himself, merely his minion and not worth the effort of running from. Stay put, sir, stay put.

> EARL *walks into the quarry. He is a full-bearded tramp dressed in voluminous clothes that fall about him, which along with his beard and hat so cover him that it is difficult to pick out his features, except for his sharp and mobile eyes. There is jauntiness in his walk and sparkle in his voice. He stops by the car.*

EARL: As I say, a fine and lofty view you have from here. I admire your choice of resting place. And whom have I the honour of addressing?

LUKE: The name's Luke.

EARL: And mine Earl. (*He shakes hands elaborately.*) Known by such to both my friends and my enemies. Makes life easier. You can love me and call me Earl, or you can hate me and call me Earl, and I shall never know the difference. Two names are a nuisance.

LUKE: Are you on the road?

EARL: I am, as you so delicately put it, young man, on the road. Not a respected nor much followed profession nowadays, but still (*he eyes the car*) one of great rewards. Is this your car?

LUKE: Yes, mine. Ours really. Some friends and me is doing it up, see?

EARL: Ah! You've friends. You and your friends?

LUKE: Friends? Yes ... suppose so. (*The idea gives him pleasure.*) Yeah, me and my friends.

EARL: Indeed. Doing it up? How sad. Nothing is left to die comfortably and alone nowadays. Someone always wants to patch and mend. It's a bothersome world. Truly a pity. That car would have made a nice berth for the night.

LUKE: That's what I've been using it for – sleeping in.

EARL: Indeed? (*He stands looking, obviously waiting for an invitation to use the car too.*)

LUKE (*realizing at last*): Oh! You can share it if you like.

EARL: May I? What generosity! (*He climbs into the back seat.*) Yes, indeed. Two could manage comfortably. One in the front and one in the back.

LUKE: O.K. Only tomorrow my friends and me will be doing it up so you'll have to help or keep out of the way.

EARL: But of course, I never hinder. There's too much to do in the world to waste time hindering. I said to my last employer – I occasionally give of my services, you know? – I said to my last employer, I never hinder men at work. I'm glad to say he took the hint. He sacked me that night. Very accommodating chap like that. Said he wouldn't hinder me from moving on. (*He leans confidentially close to* LUKE.) There is, however, one problem with the generous arrangement we have just made.

LUKE: What's that?

EARL: The back seat is far more comfortable than the front.

LUKE: Then we'll have to take turns at sleeping in the back, won't we?

EARL: Admirable suggestion. Very sensible. I'd hate to deprive you of your sleep by leaving you in the front every night! (*They laugh together.*) Come, my friend. You must tell me about yourself. A young apprentice to the fellowship of the road – most unusual: at least in the professional sense. Plenty of these thumbers who cadge lifts and take rides. But *real* – pardon the expression – tramps! There's few of us left, and youngsters rarely join us nowadays.

Aidan Chambers

Acknowledgements

The authors and publishers wish to thank the following for permission to reproduce copyright material. It has not been possible to contact all copyright holders, and the publishers would be glad to hear from any unacknowledged copyright holders.

Jonathan Cape Ltd and Roger McGough for 'Nooligan' and 'Streemin' from *In the Glassroom* and 'Snowscene' from *Watchwords* by Roger McGough; Curtis Brown Limited and Neil Paterson for 'Three Fingers are Plenty' from *And Delilah*; Aberdeen College of Education for 'Out of Place' by Colin Smith and 'It May be Necessary to Apply a Second Coat' by Lesley Rigg from *The Fifth Estate*; Robert Morgan for his poem 'Maladjusted Boys'; Macmillan, London and Basingstoke, for extracts from *Dragon in the Garden* by Reginald Maddock and the poem 'Elephant' from *Brownjohn's Beasts* by Alan Brownjohn; A D Peters & Co Ltd, and Ray Bradbury for the extract 'All Summer in a Day' from *A Medicine for the Melancholy*, originally published in Fantasy and Science Fiction Magazine. Iain Crichton Smith for his poem 'Rythm'; Faber and Faber Publishers for the extract from *Lord of the Flies* by William Golding; A M Heath & Company Ltd, David Walker and Collins Ltd for 'The Advertisement' from *Geordie*; IPC Magazines Ltd for 'I Want to be England Manager — Peter Shilton Speaks' adapted from *Shoot* magazine; Margaret Ramsay and Willy Russell for the play 'The Boy with the Transistor Radio' [All rights whatsoever in this play are strictly reserved and application for performances etc. should be made before rehearsal to Margaret Ramsay Ltd., 14a Goodwin's Court, St. Martin's Lane, WC2. No performance may be given unless a licence has been obtained.]; Collins Publishers for the extract from *In and Out of the Box* by Robert Dougall; Jenny Joseph for her poem 'Warning' from *Rose in the Afternoon* (J.M. Dent 1974); Andium Press for 'Note for the Future' from *A Single Flower* by Jim Burns; Adam McNaughtan for his poem 'Skyscraper Wean' from *The Scottish Folksinger*; EMI Music Publications and International Music Publications for 'Back Buchanan Street' by H. & G. Dyson © 1967 Robbins Music Corp. Ltd.; W H Allen & Co for 'On Saturday Afternoon' from *Sillitoe Selection* by Alan Sillitoe; James MacGibbon for the poem 'Not Waving but Drowning' from *The Collected Poems of Stevie Smith*, published by Allen Lane; William Heinemann Ltd for the extract from *Of Mice and Men* by John Steinbeck; Watson, Little Limited for the poem 'The Rebel' by D J Enright, published by Chatto & Windus; Martin Secker & Warburg Ltd for the poem 'Suicides' from *Selected and New Poems* by John Hall; A D Peters & Co Ltd and Roger McGough for the poem 'Let Me Die A Youngman's Death' from *The Liverpool Scene* published by Donald Carroll; Houghton Mifflin Company for the poem, 'The Plaint of the Camel' from *Admiral's Caravan* by Charles Edward Caryll; Vicki Feaver for her poem 'Slow Reader' from *Strictly Private*; Radio Times for 'New Readers Begin Here' from the launch of *On the Move*; London Express News and Features Services for the article 'The Gypsies' by Lewis de Fries; Newsweek for the article 'We Have Never Been Free' by Howard Lawrence; Heinemann Educational Books for the extract from the play *The Car* by Aidan Chambers; The New Yorker Magazine Inc. for 'The Test' by Angelica Gibbs © 1940, 1968; Willow Music and Warner Brothers for 'Ledge Psychology' by Bob Newhart; George Allen & Unwin (Publishers) Ltd for 'The Lapse' by Alun Lewis from *The Last Inspection and Other Stories*.

Illustrations
Tony Hudson: pages 2, 16, 47, 60, 94 and 103;
Tessa Barwick: pages 22, 25, 80, 82 and 83;
Leaper and Gard: pages 4, 7, 9, 31, 34, 51, 67, 70, 73, 84-5 and 87;
Barnaby's Picture Library: pages 36, 53, 54, 55, 56, 76, 77, 91, 99, 100 and 101;
BBC Copyright Photograph: page 40.
Photo Source: page 36.